WANTED BY ELVIS

KIDNAPPED BY BATMAN

CAPTURED BY WARREN

Hollywood 1961-1964
Echo Park to the Sunset Strip

By:

Bonnie Karlyle aka Karen Conrad

Hot Ticket

ISBN: 9798853840614
ISBN- 10: 1477123456

Cover design by Michael C. Karlyle
Library of Congress Control Number TXu002366793
Printed in the United States of America

TABLE OF CONTENTS

ACKNOWLEDGMENTS

First comes my children, who were always first in my heart and mind. Robin Pollock Jacobs, Chris Pollock, Michael and Randy Karlyle, and their wives and girlfriends. Especially Michael, who was my savior when it came to any technical help.

My "Friends and the 'Serendipity Angel" on my shoulder: Lyndie Wenner for her brilliant suggestions; Juanice Charmaine, who shared my "Book Birthing" with me along with Jake Wallick, my "Goodfella," Sharon Brooks, Jeannie Moore, and Carol Goddard, and especially my Budd Albright, my friend from the "Hollywood Days." Who shared his 'Kart,' knowledge, and memories from the past with me for this book. Thanks go to Maria Stuart for her help.

INTRODUCTION

I knew the odds were against me, a divorced twenty-year-old with two babies under the age of four, trying to escape a life that started with an abusive stepfather and was now on the run from the fate of a life in a small town with an abusive ex-husband.

I had promised myself, come hell or high water, I would live the life I had always dreamed of, and now I was making my way down the California I-10 freeway to the city with the Hollywood sign on the hill.

Reality set in 15 miles down the busy road as my daughter, Robin, and I sang along with Elvis's "It's Now or Never" playing on the radio. My youngest, Chris, slept soundly, lost in his baby boy dreams under his blue blanket on the back seat.

Suddenly, my newly purchased used dream car, said to be in perfect condition by the lying salesman, took its last gulp of gas and drove its last mile. I pulled over safely to the side of the road. I got out, walked around the car, and lifted the hood. My heart sank. I knew all about blown engines from my ex, and I realized my new car's demise.

A tear fell on the hot engine, and I watched it sizzle; while holding back a hysterical giggle, I weighed my options: Should I call home? Should I go back? I couldn't do that.

Lost in my dilemma while calming Robin down, I looked up as a highway patrol officer pulled up to my rescue, asking if I needed help. What I needed was a miracle, but all I had was this man telling me what I already knew: the engine was blown.

"Can I take you to a phone booth so you can call your husband?" he asked, rocking back and forth with his hands in his pockets.

I didn't have to think long about that.

"Nope, please take us to the nearest bus station," I said as I turned to grab what I could from the car, gathered the kids, wiped the last tear from my face, and then locked the car doors.

We were going to Hollywood. There was no turning back, car, or no car. We were taking the bus.

SERENDIPITY: IS THE LUCK OF FINDING YOURSELF IN THE RIGHT PLACE AT THE RIGHT TIME

My life has taken me from San Francisco to Echo Park to Hollywood and the big screen. All along the way I met so many people, some wonderful, some not, and made many friends, each teaching me lessons about life and myself.

Then, when I stood on the cusp of realizing my Hollywood dreams, I decided to walk away.

To appreciate where I landed, you need to understand how I learned to fly.

This is my story…

PROLOGUE: SOUTHERN CALIFORNIA, FEBRUARY 2023

Hail bounced off the windshield of my car as I pulled into the driveway after enjoying lunch with my close friend, Judy. The radio was playing an Elvis song, "Until It's Time for You to Go." Dark gray clouds hung heavy in the sky, and thunder shook the earth beneath my high-heeled boots.

California was in the midst of an unusual storm, one that would last for days and one that was desperately needed as the area had been on the cusp of a major drought. I was freezing from the unseasonably chilly weather as I raced up the steps to my warm house. The words of Elvis's song kept running through my head as I opened the door.

> You're not a dream
> You're not an angel
> You're a woman
> I'm not a king
> Just a man
> Take my hand
> We'll make a space
> In this life that we planned
> And here we'll stay
> Until it's time for you to go.

Those words took me back to the Spring of 1964 when Elvis Presley took my hand. "Come on, baby," he said. "Let's get away from these loud guys and girls. I'd rather be alone with YOU." Then he led me down the hallway to his dimly lit bedroom and closed the door.

1.   "Until It's Time for You to Go" lyrics written by Buffy Sainte Marie © Howe Sound Music Publishing LLC)

SAN FRANCISCO, CALIFORNIA 1943

My first memory is of my mother, June, putting me into a crib with a screened, wooden frame top that closed. I can still see her standing above me, lowering the top so I could not escape.

We were on the 10th floor of a San Francisco hotel, where she had come to be with my stepfather-to-be, Bill Conrad, a short-tempered man who was on leave from the Navy.

As the story goes, I had found my way to the sill of an open, unscreened window. I think I was trying to escape because I was not thrilled with my mother's choice for her next husband. But had it not been for that man's quick thinking, I would not be here today because as I made my way to the open window and a 10-floor fall to the ground, he reached out, grabbed my dress, and pulled me to safety.

Even though he was not the father I would have chosen, I should at least thank him for saving my life.

That event was a sign of my independent, fearless, gypsy soul: perhaps it is because I was caged in that box of a crib that I have feared being tied down or closed all my life.

I was born Bonnie June Ayres. My real father was James Ayres; my mother married when she was nineteen and divorced him when I was two.

Then my mother married the about to become abusive Bill. I couldn't wait to get away from that man and my escape came when I got married at fifteen.

SILVERLAKE, CALIFORNIA 1941-1945

Panorama Terrace

My first five years were mostly spent living with my grandparents: "Sweetie," the nickname I used for my grandmother, whose real name was Norma; and my grandfather, Hugh Boyd, who we called "Poppy." They met after Poppy graduated from Stanford University, where he studied English literature.

Sweetie and Poppy were married in Watsonville, California, around 1920. My mother, June, was their firstborn; then came my uncle Doug, and lastly, Lorna, my aunt. Sweetie and Poppy built their home on a corner lot in the Silverlake neighborhood of Los Angeles. It was a

Spanish-style house, kind of an L-shaped dwelling with a red tile roof and a white stucco exterior. Sweetie had beautiful plants in the front yard, gardenias and pretty purple iris, and these dainty fuchsias that I pretended were ballerinas and made them dance as I hummed some pretty tune.

The back courtyard stepped down to a walled garden with a built-in Spanish-tiled fountain. It was my very own "Secret Garden," which I named after the classic Frances Hodgson Burnett "The Secret Garden," which Sweetie had read to me. I could open a wooden gate to a lot between our property and that of our neighbor, which was partly filled with wild growth. I played with the neighbor's son there, and Sweetie planted vegetables in a cleared area.

One day, on the way out to her vegetable garden, Sweetie lost her little silver stork scissors that she had put in her apron pocket. I tried to help find them by going back and searching the path we had walked on. Sweetie told me that finding them would be like "finding a needle in a haystack." I said I would find them for her if it took all day. I searched and searched in the weeds all around the garden area until I found them; I can still see Sweetie's face beam when I handed them to her. I have such sweet memories of those early days with her.

The inside of the house was decorated in California Spanish style with glazed painted tiles around the fireplace, terracotta tiled floors, and Mission-style furniture.

Boyd's Thanksgiving

I remember the ritual of drawing the heavy blackout curtains in the rooms at night because we were at war with Japan after the bombing of Pearl Harbor in 1941. The war lasted until 1945.

Poppy was the vice principal of boys at John Marshall High in Los Angeles. He was so well-loved there that the football field was named for him; when it was renamed again years later, the track field then bore his name.

Poppy was in his late forties in 1949 when he died of a heart attack. So many people came to his funeral to say goodbye that there wasn't any room left to sit at Forest Lawn Cemetery in Glendale.

ECHO PARK, LOS ANGELES, CALIFORNIA 1945-1950

Bill and Bonnie

Bonnie

I became a child of summer in the mid '40s, when my mother married the mean-spirited Bill after the war. We moved to 1120 Echo Park Blvd., where Bill's family owned a four-plex and where the park and lake were almost at our doorstep. I spent most of my time outside, brown as a berry, barefoot, and loving every minute I could spend near the water.

I had a new baby brother, Billy, born with cerebral palsy and requiring extra care. Billy was a beautiful, sweet boy with dark hair, big blue eyes, and dark lashes who brought a change to our lives. My mother took him on the bus three times a week for physical therapy at The Children's Hospital. Bill, devastated by his son's diagnosis, became even meaner.

There was a steep flight of stairs from the sidewalk to the front porch, one entrance leading to the two first-floor apartments, and another stairway to the two apartments above. We lived high above the street with a view of part of Angelus Temple that sat at the far end of Echo Park Lake.

I could hear church music coming from the temple, and I never failed to cross paths with one of the members. "Little girl, have you been saved?" they asked as they tried to convert me when I was just six, but I was destined to be Catholic; before marrying Bill, my mother had a Catholic boyfriend, and she decided I should be baptized Catholic. And so it was that I quickly learned about sin and hell and all the scary things the church, with its Latin masses, instilled.

I faithfully rose every Sunday morning for Mass at Our Lady of Loretto on Union Street. I refused to eat meat on Fridays, and I said my Hail Mary's every day, like a good Catholic child. I slept with a picture of Jesus over my bed, and I remained the only one in my family to practice my religion.

I still have a picture of me, a sad-looking, skinny child in a virginal, white dress and veil on the day of my First Communion. When I wasn't reading about Christ, I was outside, running up and down the stairway from the street to our apartment.

***

I had a lot of room to roam, which I did every afternoon as my mother went to work before I got home from school. I entered my make-believe world and played under the foliage and trees, with their wonderful hiding places. I played house with my dolls and was the best mother they could have.

I roamed the vacant lot next door. I smelled and tasted the wild fennel plants growing amongst the weeds and flowers; I found the trap door spiders burrowing beneath the ground, making their tunnels, and closing the little doors that let them in and out; I walked to the lake and played by the feathery cream plumes and fuzzy brown pussy willows that grew by the water's edge. I ran barefoot through the wet, green grass; sometimes, I saw fish poke their heads through the muddy lake and water lilies, and I fished for them with my homemade stick and string pole.

One day, I got lucky and caught a big catfish. I dragged it home and pleaded with my mother to let me keep him. He was a tough old fish that survived the trip out of the water, and he swam happily in my tub for a few days until I was made to take him back to the lake and set him free.

At the park, I saw winos passed out on park benches or the ground, covered with dirty coats or tattered blankets, empty bottles, and crumpled paper bags filled with their worldly possessions, sometimes by their side. Though the park was not the best place for a child to roam, even back then, I now realize I was often safer there than in my home with my abusive stepfather, Bill.

I also had to watch for broken glass as I made my way to the Pioneer Market on the corner of Sunset and Echo Park Avenue to buy a treat or look at the pretty Story Book dolls.

The market gave the dolls away if you collected enough pink cash register receipts. I loved collecting those beautiful little dolls, with their big, open eyes and fancy costumes from foreign countries. My favorite was the doll from Holland with her wooden shoes. (Oh, how I longed for a pair of my own. How did one ever walk in wooden shoes? Sweetie told me that her side of the family came to

Roxbury, Massachusetts, from England via Amsterdam, Holland in 1635.)

I was brave enough to go door-to-door, asking strangers for their pink slips. An elderly lady once said, "I'm sorry honey, I only wear white slips." So, I revised my little speech to add that I was collecting the pink grocery slips from the market.

I was a brave little thing. I had no fear of going door-to-door and talking to strangers. My life at Echo Park was interesting, to say the least.

***

My first love was ballet. I took lessons from the age of seven to fifteen. During my Echo Park years, I studied with a Russian teacher named Theodore Kosloff. I got on the bus alone with my cherished pink satin-toe shoes and traveled down Sunset to Vermont Avenue to the Kosloff Dance Studio. There, we would line up at the bar and do our exercises while our teacher sat in a throne-like chair, tapping his stick while saying in his Russian accent, "Girls 1, 2, 3," to the rhythm of the practice music playing on the record player. He was a big, muscled man with shoulder-length grey hair and a beard. His strong, rough voice alone kept us in line.

He wore a tan leather headband and often tapped our legs with his cane to correct a wrong move. "Tighten that leg; higher, higher, lift that leg higher," he'd say. "No, no, your arms need to float like this. You're too stiff." I loved the discipline. Later, my mother told me that she read in the paper that Mr. Karloff's brother, Alex, had been arrested for making 'improper' movies.

Theodore Kosloff was also an actor and choreographer in his early years in Hollywood until talkies became popular, and he was given a star on the Hollywood Walk of Fame.

Every night, I closed the door in the living room, turned on my beautiful ballet music, and pretended I was Pavlova. I danced until I was told to take my bath and get ready for bed.

***

Saturdays in Echo Park were mostly spent at the movie theatre on Sunset Boulevard, which was within walking distance of our home. I loved the movies, even the newsreels, and all the serials that would keep us on the edge of our seats and coming back week after week to see what happened next.

Sweetie had moved to Glendale and would come and take me to the local theatre to see wonderful musicals, like "Oklahoma," "Carousel," and "South Pacific," after which I would play act and sing on the way home.

***

My education began at Logan Street School, which was about four or five blocks away. To get from the schoolyard to the playground across the street, we had to walk through a scary tunnel.

The best thing about the Logan Street Grammar School was a program that bused kids downtown for ballet or opera performances in the big, beautiful theaters. I'm sure this helped light my desire to dance and act.

My best friend in school was a Black girl named Karen. My stepfather was not thrilled that my best friend was Black, but as stubborn as I was, she stayed my best friend and was the first of many Black people I would become close to during my life. This was the '40s, and I would prove to be a rebel child standing up to the injustice I would see throughout the years. I later became a dancer traveling with Art Laboe's "Oldies but Goodies Show," and I saw how much bigotry there was outside my small world.

***

I was born with wispy, drab, brown, mousy hair that wouldn't stay put, no matter what my mother did, so she decided to perm it.

Those days, perming was done by a machine with a hood and curlers hung from wires that were rolled into your hair. The machine was enough to scare any child, and I cried when I was put through this torture.

I cried every time I looked in the mirror and saw my short, tightly curled hair. It looked awful. I wanted my hair long and straight, but my mother did not like long hair. We never would agree on hairstyles. Until the day she died, her hair was mostly kept short.

I was ten when my mother took me to The May Co. on Wilshire Boulevard. It was my first visit to a department store, and we were shopping for my first bra. I wanted to grow up fast so I could wear the pretty clothes like those hanging on racks and the beautiful outfits the mannequins wore in the colorful window displays.

***

My mother woke me on one Echo Park morning in
1949.

"Come see what's outside," she said.

I climbed out of bed and ran to the window. Something
white blanketed the vacant hill next door. It was my first
snow: beautiful, glistening gold in the morning sunlight and
turning wet, icy, and dirty in the afternoon.

***

The girls at Logan Street School in 1950 were all too
ready to grow up. When I was about nine, all they could
talk about was whether they had started their periods. None
of us really knew about the birds and bees, but we tried to
act way older than we were. A few of the girls said they had
gotten their periods; I had not and was teased endlessly.

One day, I took a sanitary pad from my mother's box
and my little pink belt that I was saving for the big day and
wore it to school so I could say I had started my period. I
had a pomegranate in my lunch bag, and after getting
teased again, I went to the restroom, closed the door on the

stall, and smashed a few of those red seeds on my pad. I gleefully came out and lied about "becoming a woman."

More than a year later, on New Year's Eve, I had the big day. I was home alone, curled up on the couch in our new home in Glendora, going through my first case of bad cramps, which made me wish I hadn't been so anxious to become a woman.

GLENDORA, CALIFORNIA 1951

Glendora in the early '50s, was a small bedroom community with a lot of smudge pots and orange trees with sweetly fragrant flowers, things I'd never smelled in the city, along with some narrow-minded people as far as I was concerned.

Glendora was next door to another small town called Azusa, which was mainly Hispanic. There was some unmarked line dividing the two cities and their residents, though they shared the same high school and small community college.

The good people of Glendora told my parents: "Don't let your daughter associate with the kids from Azusa." They had no real knowledge of where I had come from, as Echo Park was the melting pot of L.A. The rebel in me just needed to hear "don't," and I did.

So, my parents were disappointed that instead of joining the popular girls in my grammar school, I chose to hang out with what Bill called the "underdogs."

Glendora was supposed to be the perfect place to raise a child. Well! I would learn in the next few years that the police captain was molesting his own daughter. A girl I knew in school was pregnant by her father. Couples cheated on each other, and child abuse was happening right under the righteous noses of these so-called good, proper people.

I guess some people did better burying their heads under orange tree leaves than facing the fact that they were really living in another "Peyton Place," or maybe the "smudge" from the smudge pots had clouded their judgment.

My mother went to work at the bank in Covina during the day so she could be home at night, and Billy Jr. started a special school.

***

Life would be different in Glendora. I was alone during the day and often walked downtown, which was about six blocks from our house. "Town" was two blocks with buildings and shops.

This was a very small town, not at all like the city I had been raised in. It seemed most people living there at that time were from Arkansas or Oklahoma, and they talked with different accents, ones I never heard in LA.

Old men sitting on benches in front of the barbershop, or the coffee shop stared at me as I walked to the high school swimming pool to cool off during the hot summers. Workers building new houses on the street when we moved in stared and made comments when I left the house or played in the yard. Things were different in Glendora, or maybe I hadn't been as aware during my Echo Park days; either way, I felt less safe in Glendora.

***

I loved art and painting faces with oil paints on canvas. In high school, I would paint the faces of sad children. My art teacher, impressed with my work, put one of my paintings on exhibit. I loved working with oils as I was able to blend and add more shadows and highlights.

I could get lost in the faces I would paint, and I almost knew what each look said, what each light in an eye and each turn of a corner of the mouth might mean if that person were to speak. I would paint off and on for many years and found that the faces I painted of Blacks said more to me than any others.

I now buried my face in books. I read "Gone with the Wind," "Jubilee Trail," and "Forever Amber." I loved historical novels, anything that took me far away from the present, and the beginning of the unwanted advances from my abusive stepfather.

When I was fourteen, a ballet studio opened in Glendora, and I was finally able to take lessons, which brought a smile to my face and helped fill my emptiness.

Life was different, and I missed Echo Park and Sweetie. I made a few friends, and I met Will, a tall, blond, blue-eyed cutie a year older than I, who became my steady boyfriend. We were together as much as we could be, and close enough that I could share my fears about my stepfather. He wanted us to marry after he finished high school. My young schoolgirl, romantic self said yes, as I thought I would be saved. I would escape the abuse in my home by getting married, as that was what girls did in the '50s. No one ever asked if I wanted to go to college or what I might do with my life. I would be a wife and have the family I always wanted.

Two years later, a man named Fred Lala came to our dance studio and wanted three girls to perform at the Women's Club. I was one of the three lucky ones.

Fred Lala was married to Sally Rand, the famous fan dancer from the '30s and '40s. They lived in Glendora, where Fred was also a building contractor.

This was my first step in show business. We performed a modern dance routine, and our mothers made costumes of satin. We had long skirts and halter tops, one-half burgundy, the other turquoise. These were a far cry from my pink tutu and toe shoes I had grown up with.

After our performance, Fred gave us each an orchid. I was given a special one that wasn't the same color as the ones the other two girls received, and the way he looked at me let me I know I was special in his eyes.

I found out the next day after our performance that I was pregnant with Will's child. My dance teacher later told the two other girls that I could have been a star and that I had ruined my life.

My life changed. I escaped from the Glendora house and Bill. I also would find out I was trading one abusive male for another in training.

MARRIAGE 1957

The few years that Will and I were married were turbulent, with increasing abuse from Will happening more and more with each year that passed.

Will and I lived with his parents for the first five months after our quickie marriage in St. George, Utah. The only picture I had of that day was a black-and-white 3x4 print of our mothers, Will and I, standing in front of a motel. The groom, dressed in jeans and a plaid shirt, and me, the bride, in black capris and a sweater, with a black scarf covering my head instead of a white veil.

Looking back, that photo should have been the first clue that my fairy tale idea of marriage might not turn out to be so rosy.

I babysat for two young boys, walking about three miles to get to their house during the week to make an extra ten dollars. Will's mother, Rita, let me use her sewing machine to make my maternity tops out of cheap cotton fabric that had to be ironed each time one was worn. I remember one top was a tiny green-and-white check material and another with a light blue printed eyelet pattern that had been my favorite. I had a pair of black capris with a stretch middle for my growing tummy. I loved being pregnant and was on cloud nine planning our life and the family I'd always wanted.

Just before our first child was born, Will and I rented a small apartment. Will had a job working full-time after he graduated from high school. I promised my mother I would go back to night school and get my high school diploma, which I did.

I still had to babysit to earn extra money. Our budget was tight, and money was always a problem when extras came along. We would count our pennies to celebrate something and buy a pizza when we'd saved enough or go to a drive-in movie for a night out and maybe share a big bag of popcorn.

When I was nine months pregnant, during one of the many verbal fights we had after moving to our own place, Will grabbed me around the neck while yelling at me. Then he banged my head against the bedroom wall as I pleaded for him to stop. Our neighbor started yelling, "If you keep this up, I'm going to call the police." Thankfully, Will stopped.

The next time he grabbed me by the neck, I was in the kitchen, and I grabbed the frying pan I was about to fry chicken in and threatened to hit him over the head if he didn't let go. He turned, swore, and left, slamming the door behind him. My tears fell as I finished frying the chicken, which I ate alone at our little chrome kitchen table for two.

I had taken home economics in middle school, which at that time was a requirement for the girls as shop was for the boys. I found I loved cooking. As Will's wife, I would make Spam ham, which was a faux-baked ham with brown sugar and cloves stuck in it. I made a mean Baked Alaska, which at that time was a favorite ritzy desert. My favorite was cream puffs or eclairs, which to this day are my go-to when my sweet tooth cries out for a sugar fix.

Will's car was constantly breaking down, and his level of stress was building with each occurrence. The money always seemed to go to fixing his '56 Chevy with the newest rims, etc. Boys in the late '50s always had to outdo one another, and Will was still a teenage boy trying to walk in the shoes of a husband and father.

Our daughter, Robin, was born in July 1958 and was the beautiful little girl I had dreamed of. Sweetie came to help me for a few days when I got home from the hospital. I loved being a mother, reading every book I could find about raising babies while Will tried the best he could at his young age.

A year later, I was pregnant again. Out came Rita's sewing machine, along with the cheap cotton fabric that had to be ironed every time it was washed.

Back in those days, I washed diapers, baby clothes, and small items by hand until I was able to acquire someone's old wringer washing machine. It sat outside the back door, where a clothesline hung from the house to a tree so I could hang everything out to dry on sunny days instead of on a standing wooden hanger in the bathtub. There were no disposable diapers in those days; it was safety pins, cloth diapers, rubber pants, and smelly diaper pails.

My first son, my sweet Christopher, was born in June 1960. I now had my little girl and boy, a perfect little family. Will was going around saying, "I have a son," and in those days, was a proud father. I hoped it would help him grow up a little more, but that was just wishful thinking.

We moved closer to his parents, and Will got another job working at night in the San Fernando Valley, but still, there were the weekend nights he would drink too much beer, and I would have to leave the apartment with my babies, diapers and bottles packed in the stroller, making that long walk in the dark to a friend's house, with tears running down my face, and bruises on my arms.

I did not find out until a few years later that Will was taking uppers to stay awake at his job on the night shift. Pills didn't go well with someone who already had a bad temper and trouble handling the pressures of a young family.

Robin & Chris

THE DREAM – A NEW CHAPTER

First professional photo taken for a billboard

An old school friend of Will's was studying to become a hairdresser and asked me to be his model. My hair was bleached blonde, and I made movies for the cosmetology school and modeled at hairdresser shows. I loved getting out in the world. At home during the days, I started ironing dress shirts to make extra money. One young man felt so sorry for me that he paid me extra but decided the cleaners would do a better job, so that didn't last long.

My hair changed colors almost as often as Will changed moods. I modeled one night on the weekend when Will was home to babysit. The teacher, Duane Davis and two other students, and I decided to drive to Las Vegas one night after a show. "Come on, ladies. Let's go have some fun," he said as we stopped at the gas station to fill up his car. I called Will from the pay phone.

"Will, Mr. Davis is taking us to Vegas to celebrate, and he promised he'd have us home before the kids get up. Hope it's O.K."

Will was half asleep and muttered, "All right."

I had never been to Las Vegas. This was my first taste of doing something outside the box. We had a ball and Mr. Davis, with his big new car, was very impressive. After my divorce he and I became very close, and we remained friends for years.

***

I entered a beauty contest at the Pomona Fairgrounds. I didn't win, but we were to model in our swimsuits for photographers at the photography building. I met a man who encouraged me to start modeling for extra money. It wasn't much more than a few billboards and ads, but in those days, it helped, and I was able to get photos for a portfolio. I also started working at a pharmacy during the day as Will was still working nights. He watched the kids until he went to work at three, and I had a sitter for two hours until I came home from my work. Our lives were growing farther and farther apart.

Will and I separated when Chris was three months old, and Robin was two. I had had it. I found a small, two-room apartment and kept my job at the pharmacy; later, I found work as a waitress to keep my working hours shorter.

I had two pairs of shoes and very little in the way of clothes, maybe enough to fit in a coat closet with room to spare. It wasn't much for us to move as we had very little: a bench for a couch, a T.V., a crib, a bed, and a dresser. Will was directed to pay $50 a month in child support, but that didn't last. I would find out that the courts in those days did little to enforce child support.

I walked my babies in the stroller to a babysitter. I washed the diapers and baby clothes by hand or took them in the stroller to the laundromat. I had no car, but I must say I had guts. I was 18 at the time, and life was mine for the taking. I had guts but no money.

I managed to support my babies, although now I don't know how I made it.

I certainly was still very naive during my job at the pharmacy. I loved working in the cosmetics section, but I had to also help customers in the other departments. I was trained to ask a customer what the item was to be used for if I didn't know what the item was.

One day, I approached a man who seemed lost and asked, "Can I help you find something, sir?" He looked a little embarrassed, and I then asked my question: "What is it used for?" The item was a prophylactic, in other words, a rubber. He turned and walked out of that store to go where he wouldn't be embarrassed by a young girl.

A few months after we separated, Will's mother, Rita, came to see me, upset and almost in tears. She shook her head and said, "I don't know how to tell you this, but Will's gotten a sixteen year-old girl, also named Bonnie, pregnant.

"Her parents are threatening to put him in jail if he doesn't marry her," Rita said with tears in her eyes. "Bonnie, he's still in love with you and he hoped to get back together. He's so upset that he can't stop crying, and I just don't know what to do."

I was surprised when she asked, "Honey, could you please help and talk to him."

I was shocked and angry. I did not want to go back to him, but I said I would talk to him, and he came over, a broken, crying mess of a boy of nineteen. I held him as he cried in my arms; after, we had sex for the last time.

"You'll have to marry her, Will," I said. "Maybe one day we can be together again."

The least I could do was give him a glimmer of hope. I did this for his mother as she had become more of a mother to me than mine had ever been. We remained close until the day she died.

A few years later, Will was caught bringing drugs across the border from Mexico and spent three years in a federal prison.

Rita was my savior when it came to raising Robin and Chris. She was always there for us, babysitting, taking the kids on summer trips, always supporting me and my endeavors in life, and to this day she remains one of my greatest blessings.

***

I had no training for office work, but because of a high school friend I was hanging out with at the time, I was given a job in a home remodeling company that was opening a branch in Covina. I quit my job at the pharmacy and started working at my new job. I bought a car from my aunt Lorna for $50, an old, dark blue four-door with a running board. It was as big as a boat, but it got me where I needed to go to the babysitter and to work.

HOLLYWOOD BECKONS – CHUBBY CHECKER
Art Laboe's "Oldies but Goodies" 1961

One morning, as I was unlocking the door of the office, a man stopped me and introduced himself.

"I'm Joe Martin, a producer of Covina's Little Theatre, and we're putting on a play called "The Women," he said. "I think you'd be perfect for the part of Mary, the quiet, sweet one."

"Well, that sounds interesting," I said, "I would like to hear more."

I was invited to the cast meeting, and it was the beginning of a whole new world of acting. My creative side had not been active for more than a few years, but apparently, it couldn't stay hidden for long.

I met the other members of the cast, all dedicated thespians. There was Warren Vanders, a tall, handsome schoolteacher and sometime actor who was a member of The Screen Actors Guild with some acting credits. Very impressive.

Ruth was an attractive German woman, and her husband, whose name I've long forgotten, was always in the background (I think just checking up on Ruth).

Georgia was a tall, beautiful young blonde close to my age and a very good actress; I would learn she was Warren's "sometime girlfriend," although I was to later find out she liked women as well. Months later, she made a move on me and told me she would support my kids and me if I was interested, but I wasn't into that. I later would be into Warren, and he became the first of the actors with whom I would get involved.

Our acting group became a family to me. We would hear stories of "almost" getting a part in a T.V. show or a bit in a movie and stories of agents, casting couches, and jaded old men. I ate it all up. Oh, if only I could go to Hollywood and be a star, I thought.

The play and I were a success, but it would be another year before I'd take the Hollywood leap.

***

Again, one morning as I was opening the office, a cute guy about my age came from the car dealership across the street and stopped me before I finished unlocking the door.

"I've been watching you for weeks now and had to come over and meet you," he said. "You are very beautiful, and I wonder if you have ever considered being in show business? I sell cars during the day, but at night and on weekends I have a band and we need dancers. Can you dance?"

"Can I dance?" I said, "You bet I can dance."

He smiled. "I think you'll be perfect."

I ditched Will's last name, took Sweetie's last name, and was now Bonnie Boyd. I would use that name until I joined The Screen Actors Guild, where I learned there already was an actress with that name. I then professionally became Karen Conrad.

This was the '60s, and Chubby Checker and the Twist were becoming popular, and, yes, I certainly could dance. I went to Hollywood to audition for a man named Red

Gilson, who worked for the promoter of Art Laboe's "Oldies but Goodies Shows." It wasn't acting, but I thought it might be interesting. I auditioned and, with two other girls, was picked to be a Twisterette. We went on the road on weekends, traveling with the R&B groups with hit records on the radio at the time.

Candy Johnston was one of the dancers, along with another girl, Debbie, who came from back east. They were both excellent dancers, and soon we were given our costumes: gold lame stretch pants, a one-shoulder leopard-skin top, and short, low-heeled gold boots.

Even though he had a wife and four children at home, Red had a mad crush on Candy, who was just 17 but was soon to have a birthday. Candy was a virgin and fought Red off for months; he was crazy about her, and Candy telling him "No" made her more of an exciting challenge for him.

We were on our way to perform at our first show in San Diego. We met up in Covina, and Debbie's boyfriend was driving us. As we slowed to get onto the freeway, the car ahead of us slammed to a stop, and we ran into its back end.

The other car was able to pull off to the side of the road, but the hood on our car was jammed shut. Debbie's boyfriend told her to get the tire iron out of the trunk so he could open the hood. Candy and I were standing off to the side when Debbie, who was bending over the trunk to get the tire iron, got hit from behind by another car and was pinned between the two.

I'll never forget her cries of pain. All she could scream was, "My legs, my legs. How will I ever dance again?"

Candy and I didn't make the San Diego show; we were in shock for days to come. Debbie was in the hospital for months and was told she would never have her dream of a dancing career. The last we heard; she went back home to Philadelphia.

In the fall of 1961, our trio became a duo; it was just Candy and me. Our next show would now be our first, and it was at the Hollywood Palladium, where Chubby Checker was appearing with the Ray Anthony Band. I was a nervous wreck, scared to be in front of such a large audience for our first show, but I managed to get through it.

Chubby and I

The best part was meeting Chubby. He requested me to come to his dressing room after the show to be his partner for a "Hit Parader" magazine interview and photo shoot.

I loved it and felt like I had arrived. I was invited to his birthday party a few days later. I was also invited out to dinner by Ray Anthony, who drove to Covina to pick me up for dinner at La Scala in Beverly Hills. In those days, La Scala was the place to be seen. I was impressed when we were joined for dinner by a young, tan, and very handsome George Hamilton and his attractive blond date.

I don't remember her name because I couldn't take my eyes off George. Ray was much too old for me. I was about nineteen at the time, and his advances were unwelcome, and I wouldn't date him again.

Chubby was another matter. We were both Libras and really hit it off. He was so sweet and unaffected and gentle. I loved being around him. He flew me to Boston once to see his show and, during the next year or so, to Vegas. We always talked on the phone and got together whenever he came to Los Angeles. We remained close until he married a Miss World.

Many years later, we met again when I went to see him perform in Palm Springs, California. He introduced me to the audience, and we danced together one more time and had "years later" pictures taken. Once again, many more years later, we met again at a show in Oregon, where I was living at the time. I had called and left a message with his management company that I'd be there.

Chubby winked when he saw me in the audience, and later, as we talked and took our last picture, I told him that I wasn't sure he'd recognize me after all these years.

"You still look the same," he said. "I knew it was you because I'll always remember those eyes."

***

When I first met Chubby, I was living in an apartment in Covina, and my best friend was my next-door neighbor, Diane. We were into a lot of spiritual things, like sending thought waves to each other from our apartments. We were pretty good at it, and we surprised ourselves with our abilities; she'd think of an object, and I would guess what it was.

I was also able to concentrate and "will" Chubby to call me from different parts of the county when he was out on tour. I would sit with my eyes closed and picture him picking up the phone and dialing my number, and it surprised us how often he would call.

During my younger years, I would have times when I would "know things." I knew when my aunt gave birth before anyone was called.

Once, I was staying at a schoolmate's house overnight, and I dreamed that her whole family was in the living room mourning as they had lost a son. When I told her about the dream the next morning, she said, "My parents did have a son, and he died when he was only three. They never got over losing their only son."

Sometimes, I would just know.

Diane and I remained friends until the mid-'60s. She would later tell me about a man she worked with in El Monte who had gone to Mexico to meet with some people who were involved in a plot against then-President John F. Kennedy. She was frightened about what she had heard and would only tell me there was a plot.

I remembered her words when I heard the news that President Kennedy had been shot. It was also the same day my sweet brother Billy died at sixteen of a blood clot in his brain.

Back to Chubby: The last time I flew to Vegas to see him playing at the Sands Hotel, I heard one of his buddies mention another girl's name and that she was due to fly in the day I was set to leave. I was so hurt, and all I could think of was to show him I wasn't to be taken lightly.

I decided to fly home, turn around, and fly right back. I didn't know how I was going to do it, but one way or another, I was going to sit in the front row of the Sands that night and shock the hell out of him. I got back on a plane, flew back to Vegas, and called a girlfriend of mine to ask if

I could stay at her place for the night until I could leave the next morning. She said I could, and I was set.

All I had to do was get into the show and score a front-row seat. I was young, blonde, and pretty, and I guess you could say lucky. I was almost broke and didn't have the money to do what I was doing, but a handsome, dark-haired man came up to me.

"Hey, pretty lady, would you like to see the show," he asked.

"Of course," I said. "I would love to."

It turned out he had something to do with the Sands, and I was thrilled when we were escorted to a front-row seat. Talk about luck. I looked around and saw the new girl in the seat where I had sat the night before. She didn't look like all that much. I put a mysterious smile on my face and the show started.

Chubby's smile slowly faded as he saw me right in front of him in the audience. I'll never forget the look of disbelief on his face. Later, after the show was over, I heard my name paged over and over on the loudspeaker. I never picked up the phone to take his call. I took a bus to get home after spending the little money I had.

The next time Chubby was in town, he came to my house with friends of ours and took me into the bedroom to talk to me privately.

"Why did you do it," he asked.

"Do what, Chubby?"

I never admitted to what I had done. He must have thought I had a twin somewhere, as he dropped it after that.

***

Candy and I were traveling in a bus with our band, whose members were all white, and the "Oldies but Goodies" artists, who were all Black. This created a situation for me and Candy as we were both blondes and would get a lot of dirty looks and nasty comments whenever we would stop to use the restrooms, eat, or whatever. These were racist times and it hurt to see how cruel people could be. As I mentioned before, I was a rebel, and everyone was an equal person no matter what color they were as far as I was concerned.

How many people, me included, would lay out in the sun, hour after hour, to darken their skin? How could you put someone down for a darker color of skin? What was wrong with people?

I saw a lot while traveling with those groups.

On Nov. 6, 1961, we played at the Filmore Auditorium in San Francisco, and on the program were Ike and Tina Turner. I remember Tina kept to herself and stayed in the dressing room, but when she hit the stage, she put on a wonderful show that I watched from behind the curtains.

We were to drive over to Reno, Nevada, to perform the next night. As we were going over the pass during a snowstorm, the bus slid backward and came to a sudden stop. We were scared.

We were told to stay where we were in the bus, and we couldn't see anything out of the windows as it was getting dark. Later, when we were taken off the bus by the highway patrol, I saw that one back tire of the bus was hanging over the edge of the road. We apparently made the news that night.

We traveled on weekends to perform in different cities in California. We spent New Year's Eve of 1961 in California at the Long Beach Municipal Auditorium, on stage with Ike and Tina Turner, The Carlos Bros., and the Beach Boys, who were playing their first stage show. We had a great time, and everyone was very friendly and sweet, with hugs and kisses at the stroke of midnight.

I had become friends with Cleve Duncan, the lead singer of the Penguins, and his wife, Jackie. She was so sweet, and we really hit it off. I traveled with them to Texas for a show in El Paso, and we took their car instead of going on the bus with the band. Texas was not the place for a white blonde to be traveling with a Black couple as it was the Jim Crow era, and the looks came like daggers.

Candy and Red were a couple by this time, and Red was planning a career for her as a single dancer, so our time as Twisterettes was about to end. Candy went on to do a solo act, and she danced in one of the "Beach Blanket Bingo" movies.

Candy would end up married to Red, and a year or two later, I would see the happy couple during my first Palm

Springs adventure I would take with Jenny Maxwell, the actress from "Blue Hawaii." A trip where I would meet the Rat Pack along with Yul Brenner, an encounter I would never forget.

***

My life and career would take a different turn after the last show we did in Bakersfield, as we were snowed in over the Grapevine Pass with the Roger Miller Band. It was a Sunday night, and I couldn't get back to Covina to open the office on Monday morning. Fate stepped in and decreed I was to lose my day gig.

I was fired after Monday morning rolled around and we were still stranded over the pass. It was then that I knew I had to make my move to Hollywood or forever be stuck in the suburbs.

THE DREAM BEGINS 1962

That morning, I was reading a book called "The Miracle of Mind Power" by Dan Custer.

I closed my eyes and repeated the mantra I had learned from it: "I don't know what is on the way for me today, but it can only be good. I give thanks for all the good things that will come my way."

After packing up the kids and saying goodbye to their teary-eyed grandparents, I closed the car door and got behind the wheel of my new, used, yellow Chevy convertible on which I'd spend my meager savings.

With the last wave, we turned into the street that would take us to the I-10 Freeway, the road to the world of movies, stars, and exciting new adventures. Full of Hollywood dreams and loaded down with our few possessions, I left the small towns of Glendora and Covina behind on our way to the city 30 miles away.

I knew the odds were against me, a divorced twenty-year-old with two babies under the age of four, trying to escape a life that started with an abusive stepfather and was now on the run from the fate of a life in a small town with an abusive ex-husband.

I had promised myself, come hell or high water, I would live the life I had always dreamed of, and now I was making my way down the California I-10 freeway to the city with the Hollywood sign on the hill.

Reality set in 15 miles down the busy freeway as my daughter, Robin, and I sang along with Elvis's "It's Now or Never" playing on the radio. My youngest, Chris, slept soundly, lost in his baby boy dreams under his blue blanket on the back seat.

Suddenly, my newly purchased used dream car said to be in "perfect condition" by the lying salesman, took its last gulp of gas and drove its last mile. I pulled over safely to the side of the road. I got out, walked around the car, lifted the hood, and my heart sank: I knew all about blown engines from my ex, and I realized my new car's demise.

A tear fell on the hot engine, and I watched it sizzle. Holding back a hysterical giggle, I weighed my options: Should I call home? Should I go back? I couldn't do that!

Lost in my dilemma while calming Robin down, I looked up as a highway patrol officer pulled up to my rescue, asking if I needed help. What I really needed was a miracle, but all I had was this man telling me what I already knew: the engine was blown.

"Can I take you to a phone booth so you can call your husband?" he asked as he stood rocking back and forth with his hands in his pockets.

I didn't have to think long about that.

"Nope, please take us to the nearest bus station," I said as I turned to get a few things from the car, gathered the kids, wiped the last tear from my face, and then locked the car doors.

We were going to Hollywood. There was no turning back, car, or no car. We were taking the bus.

I had no real idea what we would do once we got to Hollywood, but we got there, and I found a cheap hotel room off Franklyn and Cahuenga Boulevard, where we were able to stay a few days as I looked in the want ads for modeling jobs.

I found one on the Sunset Strip, at a restaurant called The Golden Violin, modeling swimsuits at their lunchtime show, which, in the early '60s, was a popular way to build a businessmen's lunch clientele. For me, it was a way to feed my babies.

With the kids in tow, I was hired to start the following week. I had no idea what I was going to do as my car was beyond repair, but the bus worked for the time being.

After my time at the hotel was over, Sweetie invited us to stay with her in Glendale until we could save enough money to rent a place in Hollywood.

"Thank you so much for being there for me," I told her with tears in my eyes and a lump in my throat.

I found a bus that would take me from Glendale to Hollywood. Sweetie would help with the kids until I would find a sitter in Hollywood. I was going to make this work, no matter what.

***

The new job in West Hollywood turned out to be a mixed bag. The Golden Violin was dark, with wood-paneled walls, fancy gold-framed mirrors, and red booths that you had to step up to get in. A mirrored bar was across the room from the booths. Tables and chairs filled the middle of the room, leaving a walkway around the booths.

There were three other models working lunches beside me.

Babydoll introduced herself with her tiny, baby voice: "Hope you'll like it here. There's not much room in this small area where we all change outfits, but we get by," she said as she applied more mascara to her black lashes, already heavy with previous applications.

Linda shyly said hello, and Pattie told me I was pretty enough and should do well.

"The guys will like you, but stay away from my customers," she warned.

Babydoll was tall, blonde, with a figure to die for. She had big, round breasts like I'd never seen before; they were implants, as I later learned. She had a voice that was higher pitched than most, with a sweet innocence about her, hence her name.

Pattie was another matter: dark-haired, tough, and tiny; she was all business. Linda was a sweetheart, an Armenian with a strict father. She was also flat-chested and had to wear falsies to fill out her swimsuits. Later, she would get breast implants and move to Las Vegas. She and I, both the newbies and the innocents of the group, became friends. She even helped me with the kids at times.

The owner of the Golden Violin was Rose, a tough broad who had taken pity on me and was kind enough to give me a job. She had a good heart. If you pictured a floozy, Rose would be it. She always had a cigarette hanging out of her wrinkled lips, and she was probably a few sheets to the wind, but she and her husband, Al, were sharp businesspeople.

I would later learn they owned a strip club down the street called The Body Shop and had done well with their Sunset Strip businesses.

"Honey," she would say, "you're here to look pretty and get these men to hand over all the money you can get. Better you get it than someone else. Take it from me, girlie."

There was a bank on the corner of Clark and Sunset. In a few years, it would become the Whiskey A Go Go, and the Sunset Strip would be the place to be seen. Next door to the Golden Violin was a small, narrow bar called The Opera House.

A Hamburger Hamlet was on the other corner, where all the young actors would hang out during the day. Marilyn Monroe lived just a few blocks near Doheny and Sunset. I knew crimes were going on, but not like now. I would spend three years in this town, love it, and treasure every memory.

Later, when I had a car, I felt safe enough to drive down Sunset Boulevard late at night to the beach in Santa Monica, where the swings were. I'd get on that swing, and I'd swing back and forth under a blanket of stars while hearing the constant sound of the ocean waves as they would crash; somehow, it all made me feel at peace.

***

Looking back, I had just one bad casting-couch experience: A well-known casting agent for a major movie stood up from his desk after I introduced myself. He unzipped his pants, took his penis out, and asked, "What are you going to do with it?"

"Can't say it's been nice meeting you and your little friend," I said as I turned and walked out the door.

***

The job at the Golden Violin was a means to an end. I didn't want to spend my life modeling bathing suits and the baby doll nighties Rose would later decide we had to wear.

The kids and I were staying in Sweetie's tiny sewing room. The kids shared a twin bed mattress on the floor, probably the same mattress she would pull out from under her and Poppy's walnut antique bed for me to sleep on when I was a child.

I would sleep on the couch in the living room. It was not easy for Sweetie with my two little ones, but she was there for me, and that was all that mattered. Her love and strength saw me through many difficult times, and I will miss her always.

I would get up in the morning, feed the kids, kiss them goodbye, and walk to the bus stop around the corner at 9 a.m. It would take a good hour and a half to get to West Hollywood. This was my routine for the next few weeks until I could save enough money to move.

I found a converted upstairs furnished apartment above an old Italian couple's house on Clark Street, up from where I worked on Sunset. I was able to move us via the bus.

We finally had a place of our own.

I found a babysitter, and things were easier, but paying the rent was difficult as Will was not reliable with the child support. After a while, there wasn't any place in town that would cash the checks from him because they bounced so often.

I became close friends with Fred, one of the owners of the Opera House, the charming bar next door where I would stop after work to visit.

Fred was tall with blond, wavy hair. He reminded me of Ashley from the movie "Gone with the Wind." Mark Dempsey, an actor, was Fred's co-owner who may have been related to the prizefighter Jack Dempsey, who used to booze it up there almost every night.

It never entered my mind there could be more to the relationship between Mark and Fred, but Mark acted a little strange about Fred and I becoming closer and spending time together.

Later I realized that they were probably lovers, something about which I knew nothing about, even though I was in my early twenties. It broke my heart because I adored Fred, and he would say that he loved me and the kids as if they were his own. He took us out for walks and ice cream. He was such a plus to our lives.

I was still naive and way too trusting. This would be another learning experience during my Hollywood years.

KIDNAPPED BY BATMAN – ADAM WEST

I met so many interesting people during my time at the Golden Violin. After I got over being nervous about parading around in swimsuits and lingerie, I learned that most of the men were nice and not just lechers. Most knew I was a mother supporting two kids, as I never hid that. I hoped it would make them think twice about making a pass, but who knows if that ever had an effect. It became fun, and I met some interesting people.

The talented pianist and comedian Victor Borge was always a gentleman, very funny, charming, and continental, and he would come in often. Some of the customers were in show business, and some were not, and I was bad at recognizing people. There were a few people who were insulted that I didn't recognize them.

One day, a tall, handsome man came in. I had no idea who he was and felt embarrassed when he told me he was

Adam West, who played Batman on the T.V. series. He was charming, and he asked me to go out to dinner with him.

"O.K., but I have two children and will have to get a babysitter," I told him.

"Great," he replied.

We made a date for the following Friday night. I was excited for my first Hollywood date. I lined up a sitter to come over and watch the kids.

I knew I could learn so much about the business from a working actor. But acting wasn't a lesson he would teach me. Not being too trusting was a lesson I would come to learn with time and experience.

Adam picked me up in his Cadillac. I listened intently while he told me about what was going on in his career. Then I noticed he was driving away from town on the Hollywood freeway. We passed the Civic Center and turned onto the Santa Ana freeway. Alarmed, I asked him where we were going for dinner.

He laughed.

"It's a surprise," he said. "Don't worry."

He kept on driving and going on about his life, and I would occasionally try to cut in and make small talk as he kept driving and talking.

We had to be somewhere near Santa Ana when I really started getting worried.

"Adam, I have the kids with a sitter and can't be out too late," I said.

He told me not to worry. A few miles later, he suggested we turn back, but he told me not to worry.

"Adam, where are we going," I asked again. And again, he told me not to worry.

"Sweetheart, just chill out. We're going to Mexico," he said. "I'll have you back when I'm ready."

I panicked.

"Adam, my kids need me," I screamed. "Take me back home now. I have a sitter, don't you understand? I don't want to go to Mexico."

Though I begged him to turn back, he kept driving as I got more upset and closer to tears.

This man wasn't listening to what I was saying. I wasn't as worried about being with him as I didn't believe I'd end up dead or sold for slavery, it was my kids. He knew I had kids. He met the sitter at the door when he picked me up. What in God's name was he thinking?

I kept begging and was getting nowhere.

Finally, he said, "I'll call your sitter when we get there, don't worry about the sitter."

"I am worried, and I want to go back now," I yelled.

He just laughed and kept driving.

I must have said a few hundred prayers as we continued down the freeway, and God must have heard at least one because his car started heating up, and the engine started making a terrible clunking noise; it was the sound I heard when my car broke down. Adam started getting madder than hell with each grating sound the engine made.

He finally had no choice. The car was slowing, and we were barely able to safely pull over to the side of the freeway. Someone finally pulled over as he stood outside the car, looking for help. He got the man to go to a pay phone to call a taxi. I was saved from a fate in Mexico with Adam West.

My angry date had to pay for a cab to take us all the way back to the Sunset Strip to my waiting babies and sitter.

After miles of silence, he asked to see me again as the cab dropped me off at my house and I said a big "No." The cab took off with him in it. A few nights later, after the bars closed, he came to my door drunk, knocking on it and calling for me.

The landlord came to the window by my door, which led upstairs.

"Get the hell outta here," he yelled. "You're waking everyone up, you fool."

Farewell, Adam. Batman wasn't always the good guy.

THE GIRLS ON THE STRIP

The girls I met during this time were a real learning experience for a young, small-town girl. I met Miranda through a boyfriend of hers, Bob Osborn, whose younger brother, Bill, was the bartender at the Golden Violin. She was tiny, big-busted, and sandy-haired, a woman kept by a man who was one of the founders of Harvey Mudd Colleges.

She lived in a house two blocks down from Sunset. Bob was her "on the side" boyfriend. She was a sweet, caring girl with a soft, southern voice who talked about parties with Sam Yorty, the mayor of Los Angeles, as well as many other well-known people in L.A. and Beverly Hills.

She once took me to meet Henry, the older man who supported her. We had a glass of wine or two and didn't stay long. I had the feeling I was there to be checked over by Henry. She knew I struggled to keep a roof over our heads and food in the kids' mouths. She had met my kids and loved spending time with them; she wanted kids of her own someday. She also knew I wasn't going down "that road."

I don't remember how I met Bambi or who introduced us, but I now think she probably was a madam, something of which I was unaware at the time. I was invited to her house, where I was introduced to a man she said was her husband. We chatted awhile over a glass of wine before she asked me if I was interested in meeting a wealthy man to help me out.

I told her it wasn't something I wanted to do, that I wasn't desperate enough for that.

She smiled.

"If you ever change your mind, call me and I'll help you out," she said.

When I told her that I didn't think I'd be calling, she smiled.

"You never know," she said.

I smiled back and left.

Two weeks later, a friend asked me to go to an award dinner for a writer in the business. After the writer received his award, he said a few words.

"I want to bring up to the stage Bambi, the woman I have just asked to be my wife," he said. "Come on up, Bambi."

I was in shock when he announced her name. It couldn't be the same Bambi I had just met, the one who was married. But up the three steps she walked, the same tall, dark-haired Bambi I had recently met, only she was without the "husband" to whom she had introduced me.

Wow! This guy was apparently in for a con job. And I was quickly learning about another side of life in the fast lane. I decided I would just watch from the sidelines.

I met another girl on that plane ride to Vegas when I was heading back to see Chubby Checker. We were seated next to each other, and her name was Jackie Levy. Jackie was a small, beautiful, dark-haired Brigette Bardot-type girl from a wealthy Jewish family in Beverly Hills. Her father was a dentist, and she had nothing good to say about him.

She was in a rocky romance with a tall, handsome Texan. We talked about everything on that plane ride, and we stayed in touch when we were back in California.

When we met, she seemed troubled but strong. Despite her unhappiness, she advised me about men and opened up about her life. I learned that money doesn't always lead to happiness.

On that trip to Vegas to get back at Chubby, I ran into Linda, with whom I worked when I first started at the Golden Violin. Linda left not long after I started there and ended up in Vegas, where she was working as a call girl.

"I'm scared to death," she confided to me over a glass of wine. "These guys are part of the mob, and I'm afraid I might end up dead if I don't do as I'm told."

I was worried about her, so I called Bill Schindler at the Sands Hotel, the man who got me the front-row table to see Chubby's show the night before.

Bill had given me his card after I thanked him and left for Linda's apartment, telling me, "If you ever need anything, here's my card; call me." So, I called. Bill came and we all had breakfast together. Linda was able to talk to him about her problems. They really hit it off and I felt better about her having a friend in Vegas as she had felt alone. I never talked to either one of them again. I've often wondered what happened to her.

WARREN BEATTY – HAMBURGER HAMLET – A PICNIC ON MULHOLLAND DRIVE

The Sunset Strip was the place to be. I'd put the kids in the stroller and walk down Clark to Sunset Boulevard, turn right and follow Sunset for four or five blocks, cross the street, turn back and head home.

Jimmy Boyd, the singer who recorded "I Saw Momma Kissing Santa Claus," sometimes drove down Sunset in his convertible with the top down, radio blaring the latest '60s hits, waving as he passed.

The kids and I had made a few friends who worked in show business while we lived in the neighborhood.

One was Joel Kane, a writer for "Dobie Gillis," and another was Bruce Kessler, who directed "Mission Impossible" and "Hart to Hart" among others; he took me over to Ronnie Burn's house, where I met his father, the comedian George Burns, who loved his cigars and funny jokes. He was very sweet to me and, yes, a gentleman.

While seeing Bruce, I also met Lance Reventlow, a race car driver and the first husband of Jill St. John, who later married Robert Wagner, ex-husband of Natalie Wood.

Lance was going with Cheryl Holdridge at the time. I knew he was a man of wealth from the gossip columns, but I wasn't aware at the time that he was a Woolworth heir.

The Hamburger Hamlet was on the corner of Hillsdale and Sunset on the same block as The Golden Violin.

So, speaking of Natalie Wood, we would pass by while she and Warren Beatty would be sitting on the patio of the Hamlet, having either breakfast or lunch. She was as pretty as can be, with her big, fawn eyes and shiny, wavy dark hair.

Warren was a darling man/boy hunk, sweet as a southern boy could be, and talented enough to charm the pants off any girl. The two would wave, and Warren would come down and say hello to the kids and me.

He still showed up for lunch, though he hadn't been there with Natalie for a few weeks. One day, as I pushed the kids in the stroller for our walk and we came up to the Hamlet, Warren bounded down the steps like a puppy dog to say hello.

He kidded around with Robin as Chris was younger and didn't know what was going on. He turned to me with a big smile and said, "Bonnie, I think you're darling. I would like to get to know you better. Can I get your phone number?"

Here I was, a mother of two babies in a stroller, and Warren Beatty was asking for my phone number. I gave in.

"Do you have a pen," I asked.

Smiling, Warren went up the stairs to ask for the waiter's pen and a piece of paper, and then came back down the stairs to me. I promptly gave him my number. He promised to call before heading back up to finish his meal.

Warren was young, fun, and one of the nicest men I would meet. I can't say anything bad about him. I knew he had a reputation as a ladies' man, but I was twenty and flattered. I really didn't expect him to call, but he did.

Warren's first couple of calls came when I was at work. Rosie, my wonderful, funny, seventy-year-old babysitter, would answer my phone while I was gone. She and Warren had struck up a rapport, and they would joke and talk. Rosie told me he would sometimes ask to say hello to Robin because he had really taken a liking to the kids for some reason; maybe it was because he was still a delightful kid himself.

I had to turn him down a few times when I had to work, so when I answered the phone, and Rosie was there to watch the kids, he would always ask to talk to her first. Yep, that man could charm the pants off any woman, and he did.

We carried on phone conversations for a few weeks, and he began to feel like a good friend. One night, he called and asked to say hello to Rosie; then, he asked her if she would stay and watch the kids. She put me back on the phone and he asked me to take a ride with him to see a house he was either remodeling or buying. He picked me up and we drove to Mulholland Drive. He came around to open the door for me, carrying a blanket and bag with snacks and a bottle of wine in it.

The house was still being worked on, but it was big and beautiful, with a view of the valley that would work its spell on you even if Warren didn't.

But he did.

"Okay, Warren, I know you really have a crush on Rosie," I said, "I'm not jealous, but don't you think she is just a little bit old for you, buddy?"

"No, not really," he said jokingly. "I love them all."

He changed the subject to acting and the business, and then we snacked on crackers, cheese, wine, and each other. This man made me smile and laugh more than any other young guy at that time.

And that was it for us both. It was one of those delightful things you go into, knowing you should just enjoy the moment for what it is. And I did.

We still smiled, waved, and said "hello" anytime the kids and I walked by the Hamlet. As I look back at my memories, that evening remains one of my favorites. Thank you, Warren.

I'll always be thankful for our dear, sweet Rosie. That Christmas, she was worried that I didn't have presents for the kids under the tiny tree decorated with ropes of popcorn that the kids and I strung. Rosie, who loved my little family and knew we were having a hard time, always did her best to help us out. Rosie knew a man who worked at a toy manufacturing company. When Rosie was making dinner for us on Christmas Eve, I answered a knock at the door to find a tall, older man whose arms were loaded with Christmas packages for the kids, who were playing in their rooms. Rosie took the packages and hid them in a closet; she saved Christmas Day!

THE PHOTOGRAPHERS: TOM KELLY, BERNARD OF HOLLYWOOD AND EARL LEAF

My Uncle Doug called one day, saying that he wanted me to meet his photographer buddy, Tom Kelly.

"His studio is right down the street from you on Santa Monica Boulevard," he said. "You can't miss it, honey. It's that big, white building on the corner. You'll see his name on it."

He told me that he and a friend would be there for happy hour at 5 p.m. on Friday.

"Great, Dougie, sounds like fun," I said. "I can't wait to see you and catch up."

This would turn out to be my Friday hangout when I didn't have other plans or was working.

Tom Kelly was older; he was also handsome and charming. Not all that tall, he had white hair and had a down-to-earth Irish sweetness and warmth about him. I instantly felt at home in the large studio, which had a kitchen where everyone would come in and out for cocktails after Tom was done with the day's shoot at the end of the week.

Tom greeted me warmly with a big hug when Doug introduced me.

"Well, Doug was right," Tom said. "You are pretty and I'm happy to have you join our little Friday get-together. Have a seat and I'll get you a drink. What would you like?"

I smiled and asked for a Manhattan on the rocks.

We sat around the kitchen table in the area that was used for product shoots. Some of the guys leaned against the kitchen counter where Tom's helper had earlier been preparing foods for him to photograph. Usually, guys from the advertising agency would stick around for Tom's happy hour at the end of the week. You never knew who would show up, and I was told by Tom on that first Friday that I was welcome anytime.

Tom was to do headshots for me to send around to agents, but first, he wanted to send me to a hairdresser he knew to have my hair cut short and bleached. I had made a friend who worked for a clothing manufacturer and who lent me a sexy, low-cut black dress with lace at the bodice. It was beautiful; it was also something I couldn't afford. While I hated to give it back, I had to.

We arranged the evening shoot for the following week after my hair appointment, and I was on cloud nine to be getting real professional photos from Tom Kelly, the man who photographed Marilyn Monroe for her famous calendar.

The Friday before the shoot, I was again invited again to Tom's happy hour. There, I met Lindy, a regular happy hour guest.

Lindy was probably about 4-foot-8. He was very jovial and knew everyone. Lindy worked for a company that supplied background scenes for the studios, and I guess that may have been how he met Tom.

We would laugh and joke every time we would get together at Tom's. Lindy would, down the line, ask an art director at Universal Studios to see if he could get me a part on "The Virginian." I met the man; he was very nice and a perfect gentleman, and he got me a speaking part in one of the episodes as a favor to Lindy. It was nothing big, but it would give me a credit. I went in for the costume fitting and picked up a script, but two days before the shoot, I got a call.

"We're so sorry, but somebody's girlfriend had been promised the part on this episode of the "The Virginian," said the caller. "We will go ahead and pay you, but you won't be filmed."

I was crushed. I wanted that credit. But it was Hollywood, take it or leave it.

At Tom's that night, I noticed he did a little over-drinking, and with time, I would learn he had a problem. A few months or so later, he showed up at my door at about 2 a.m., drunk, slurring his words, and in no shape to drive. Thankfully, his studio was a few blocks away.

I put my arms around him to hold him steady as he mumbled, "I care about you; you know that, don't you?" "I worry…you remind me of Marilyn. You remind me of her." I let him sleep in off on my couch, and he was gone by morning.

I'm not sure, but I think he may have been in lust or love with Marilyn Monroe, maybe both. I later asked him about that remark, but he said he didn't remember.

On the evening we were to do my headshots, Tom told me I looked great.

"Wow! That black dress fits you like a glove," he said. "And I love the job they did on your hair. It's beautiful, my beautiful girl."

I felt so spoiled after my day at the upscale beauty shop in Beverly Hills. My make-up was perfect, and I was ready to go.

"Let's have a drink, and then I'll set up," Tom said. "I think we'll really get some good shots tonight. You have a face the camera will love."

It would be more than just a few drinks before he was ready. I sat on a stool while he adjusted the lighting, having me turn this way and that. When he was satisfied, he leaned over and surprised me by kissing me on the lips.

"Besides looking beautiful, you also taste good," he said. "Sweet lips, my girl."

He picked up the camera and we began.

"Okay, honey, now turn your head to the side a little," he directed me. "Ah, that's good. Yes, now look up a bit and then turn to me just a touch so the light catches your eyes. Good, yes, that's it," and on and on we went, with me changing positions and him smiling, happy with his work.

"I think we got some good ones, dear," he said. "You do photograph well, dear."

I thanked him.

"I really had fun working with you," I said. "You make it so easy, and I know how wonderful your work is. You are the best and a perfectionist at that."

Tom grinned ear to ear as he leaned over to kiss me, this time on the cheek.

"Let me make you another Manhattan, dear," he said. "I'm ready for another one."

We sat at the kitchen table, making small talk and enjoying our drinks (he probably had two more than I did), and then I told him I had to get home to my kids.

Tom walked me to the door, hugged me, and then told me with a slur that he'd have the proofs ready for me by the end of the week.

"Stop by then," he said.

I told him I couldn't wait to see them and thanked him again as I stepped out into the dark night.

I called four days later, and his assistant told me the proof sheets were ready for my review. I couldn't wait to see how they had turned out. After work, I headed to Tom's Studio, where I was greeted by the man himself, who went over to the kitchen counter, poured us a drink, and then went to the file and pulled out the envelope that held the proofs. With a grin, he pulled the sheets out as we sat down at the kitchen table.

The shots were wonderful.

"I really like this one, dear, and this one here also might be a good one," he said. "It shows your pretty, sexy eyes."

I told him it was hard to decide as I loved them all, so Tom suggested that he print up a few so I could decide at the next shoot.

It was happy hour, and with everyone else, I had a drink or two and got happy again before leaving early to get home to the kids.

The next session with Tom started out pretty much the same as the first, except this time, I wasn't wearing that beautiful black dress. It was more casual for full-body shots, and I wore Capris and a buttoned-up cardigan sweater.

The drinks were poured and poured again.

Tom would say, "I love it; oh yes, that's beautiful," as I would change positions and get on my knees and sit with my head back on a blanket, which Tom had placed on the concrete floor for me.

Tom set his camera on the stool beside him, reached over and undid some of my buttons. "Let's show that pretty shoulder of yours, dear, he said, slurring his words as he proceeded to kiss my shoulder.

We shot a few more pictures until I was in only my bra and capris. Tom and I kissed and fooled around a bit, but thankfully, Tom, having a little too much to drink, couldn't do much more, so things never went further than a friendship.

I remained close to Tom and would join the group every now and then. Years later, I took my daughter, Robin, to the studio, which Tom Jr. now ran. He had called after his father's death and was going through his father's old negatives and prints and asked if I wanted mine.

I took him up on his offer. He was sweet and charming, just like his dad, and he was taken by my pretty daughter, Robin, who would later date him.

There would be two more photographers I would meet in my Sunset Strip days. All of them had photographed Marilyn Monroe, and all three would become well known. Tom's two famous calendar shots would sell the most of any of the others; sadly, Tom always regretted selling his negatives for little money because the company he sold them to made millions.

I would meet Earl Leaf, "The Beatnik Photographer." With his black beret, glasses, and his tall, thin frame, he certainly looked the part. Earl was also a writer for "Teen" magazine, along with a few other publications in the '60s.

He lived in a white framed house with a picket fence surrounded by foliage, hidden away in the Hollywood Hills.

Earl was a sweet, giving man, and he was always a gentleman to me. He would welcome me into another world full of other young actors and actresses, some well-known and some like me, just starting out. We all loved hanging out at Earl's, where we were always welcomed.

Bernard of Hollywood was another photographer who did a lot of girlie photos. I posed for a headshot for the cover of a popular men's magazine, which paid my rent for that month.

He called me for another shoot.

"Just a few body shots a cover," he said. "I need someone new, and I think you'd be great."

I thought about it and agreed with one condition: "No full nudes."

"Got it," he said, chuckling. "I know how you feel about that."

When I got to his place, he was set up in a room, and I agreed to strip down to my panties. I draped a soft, see-through fabric down my body, and I lay on my side for the shot. There was no funny business with Bernard, thank goodness.

The magazine was called "Adam." After that, I retired from doing girlie shoots, but the check from that last job bought us food for the month.

Speaking of feeding my kids, I would be asked out to dinner by men I'd meet, and I would say yes while letting them know that I had children and would need to get a sitter.

In those days, men would offer to pay for my sitter, usually adding a little more to be impressive. That extra money helped pay for our food for a week. A mom had to do what she could to feed her kids, and that one was easy; all it would entail was a steak dinner, a goodnight kiss on the cheek, a hug, and I would take home a doggie bag.

I could always get enough change from my purse to afford gas in the car to visit my mother's house in Glendora, where I would take a few boxes of macaroni and cheese, a can or two of vegetables, or a can of tuna and Spam, which would keep us in food when things got lean.

My mother and Bill never helped me with money during those years, and she never said anything about the food disappearing from the cabinets. Those were the times of Will's bouncing checks. He and his second wife were spending their money on drugs until he was arrested for bringing them over the border.

SAMUEL FULLER LESSONS IN LIFE 1962

To KAREN CONRAD –
WHO WILL MAKE A
PERMANENT "COUP
DE FOUDRE" IN
HOLLYWOOD &
EUROPE —
LOVE &
LUCK —
Sam
Fuller
9-23-63

During my short time at the Golden Violin, I met Sam Fuller, the one man who would be in my life for most of the three years that I was in Hollywood. He was also the last one I bid goodbye to the day before I left.

Years later, in the mid-'90s, I visited him at his small apartment in Paris, France, where he lived with his wife, Christa, and his darling daughter, Samantha, who was the image of Sam.

When he greeted me at his door in Paris, he said with the sweetest, touching smile, "You remembered old Sammy?"

"How could I ever forget you?" I said truthfully as we hugged.

What a wonderful visit we had, and it was a touching ending to our friendship that began some 40 years earlier. Sam was in his eighties when I visited him in Paris, and he would die three years later.

Samuel Fuller had a passion for life and a talent that was never really appreciated in Hollywood, but he earned the acclaim he deserved in Europe during his later years, as he was considered a 'noir' writer/director.

I think it was his eyes that looked into my soul with a twinkling sparkle that I still see to this day. He was a man who was curious and would always look for and bring out the best in people. He became my biggest supporter, friend, and lover, and looking back now, probably a bit of a father figure, too.

***

When I first met Sammy, I was modeling a baby doll nightie, which I later preferred over bathing suits as it covered more. We earned a percentage of the sales of the items we modeled and sold. It sure helped this young mother of twenty to earn enough money to feed her kids.

After going through my Adam West experience, I was a little wary of dating, but Sam, with his warmth and openness, broke through my reserve. I can still see him sitting in a red leatherette booth, a cigar in his hand and a wide, crooked smile on his face. I believe Sammy was about forty at that time, which was much older than me. I had a thirst for knowledge, and Sammy came into my life to quench that thirst for both life and the past.

Years later, I would become involved in genealogy, which also entails the knowledge of history.

Sam was a writer and director. He began his career at seventeen, working as a crime reporter for a tabloid newspaper in New York City while still a high school student. Sam then turned to Hollywood and writing scripts.

Sam would be one of the first soldiers to land on Omaha Beach at Normandy during World War II. He was one of the men photographed coming off the boat in the cover picture on Life Magazine.

Sammy would work on two or three scripts at a time, with new ideas always popping up in his head. He wrote of war, crimes, and the struggles of people from all walks of life. He had a vivid imagination and a curiosity that was on 24/7. I loved this man's mind and adored his compassion for people, but the mental scars from the war were always with him. Sam made love like he was exorcising the ghosts from the past like he was still fighting a war.

There is not one bad memory from my time with Sammy.

Sam was the one who took me away from the Golden Violin weeks later. The man who worked for him as a driver/houseman was leaving, so I was given the job of shopping for groceries, running errands, and the basic cleaning of his house. I also was given an older Ford to drive, and I got to spend five days a week with Sam and his secretary, Anita Uphoff, at the large, two-story Craftsman house he rented; it was off Franklin Avenue in Hollywood, near where the large Scientology Center is now located. I would drive Anita home every night as she lived on the next block from me off the strip.

Weekends were for the kids, as I missed spending more time with them. We might drive out to Rita's and have Sunday dinner or barbequed burgers or hot dogs, as I wanted them to be around family as much as possible. Will was no longer in the picture, and Rita kept it that way due to his drug problem.

Sam later introduced me to the Bocha family, which owned The Naples Restaurant across the street from Columbia Studios, where I would hostess a few nights a week after my day job ended at Sam's, as I needed every cent I could earn.

At the Naples, I would meet the mob guys who came in from Chicago. I also met Ava Gardner, whom I thought my boss had a crush on. She was beautiful and I was in awe. I watched her and her dates drink their cocktails and eat the tasty Italian meals, followed by glasses of red wine.

There were two guys at the bar every night, Jerry and Bill were film editors who worked close by. We became friends, and a few times after work, they would buy me a glass of wine before I would head to the babysitter to pick up the kids. I was young and very impressed when these two told me that if anyone ever bothered me, to let them know.

"We'll take care of it," they said.

In this Italian atmosphere, I felt cared for and protected.

Actors from Columbia Studios would come in, like Ann Margaret, so full of energy and so beautiful. She was very friendly and sweet as well. Many actors I didn't know came in, along with writers and producers, all tired after long days on the set and who would go to the bar for a drink before heading home.

Most weeknights, the news reporters from the ABC TV Studios down the block would come in after finishing their nightly news reports. Jerry Dunphy and Bill Moyer were the two I remember most.

Bill was sweet, friendly, and a very nice man.

Jerry was handsome, with beautiful white hair and blue eyes. Sometimes, he would bring his wife in for dinner. She was a gorgeous, statuesque blonde. Jerry was always a gentleman and friendly to me; he never made a pass, so I thought he was a real family man. (A few years later, I would work at Cave De Roy, a private dining club on La Cienega, where I would run into Jerry, who turned a little red as another waitress came up to him for a hug; she later told me she was seeing him. I guess this should have been no surprise to me as, sadly, I learned that no matter how beautiful, charming, and smart a woman was, most men would make passes and probably have girlfriends on the side.)

The Naples owner, Ralph, and his wife, Connie, were sweet to me while I worked there. I was fed and sometimes given food to take home to the kids. Theirs was a real family business, and we employees were part of the family.

Ralph, trying to help me get a start in the business, once took me to meet Bobby Cohn, a nephew of Harry Cohn, at his house in the Hollywood hills. He was working as an Assistant Director at Columbia Pictures at the time. but no acting jobs ever came of the meeting.

Ralph came up to me one night while I was at the cash register and shyly gave me a packaged pair of nylons. He knew that I was the sole support of my kids at that time and couldn't afford to buy nylons. He leaned over and said, "Don't tell anyone about this." He seemed embarrassed as he was a darling grandpa figure to me.

I would have to quit the Naples when I got my first break as an actress in 1963 in Sam's movie, "Shock Corridor," with Peter Breck, Constance Towers, Gene Evans, and James Best.

Working for Sammy gave me the ability to work around interviews, photo shoots, and acting jobs and acting lessons, which Sammy arranged for me with an actor he used in many of his films.

James Best was my acting coach. In his times off from being on set, he gave acting lessons. He later gained success as Sheriff Bosco in the TV series "The Dukes of Hazzard."

I was in a class with Toni Basil, a choreographer who became successful with her hit song, "Mickey." She was related to James through his wife's family.

I remember the night she came up to me after class and said." Bonnie, when I get my nose done one day, I want a nose like yours." (I was still Bonnie as I wasn't a member of The Screen Actors Guild yet.)

I ran into her years later when I was a songwriter and was backstage at "A Salute to the American Songwriters" in L.A. I was getting the artists ready to go on stage to perform. I was talking to Thom Bell, a famous writer and music producer, as he waited his turn, and Toni walked by. Thom said hello to her, and it was apparent that something had gone down between the two of them as she gave him an icy look and turned away. I never had another chance to catch up with her, and I always thought her nose looked better than mine.

Robin and I at Sam's house in Hollywood

ACADEMY AWARDS – KEN FOLEY

I had met an attorney named Ken Foley at this time, and he became a good friend to me. He was a tall, handsome, red-headed, freckled-faced man who had been married with one daughter while he lived in San Francisco. After his divorce, he came to Beverly Hills and opened an office. Ken was a doll, but he also was an alcoholic; he was never mean when he drank; he just got quiet. He never made a pass at me, and I often wondered if he might be gay.

We would meet every few weeks for a catch-up drink at a small Italian restaurant called Dominick's on Beverly Boulevard. You pretty much had to know the owner to get in for dinner. Dom, the owner, was a kick, and Ken was a nightly customer, so it was always a good time with laughs galore as Ken and Dom kidded back and forth at the bar.

Ken called one night to tell me a client gave him tickets to the Academy Awards.

"How about it," he asked. "Would you like to go?"

"Are you kidding?" I cried. "I would love to go."

Ken told me the day and time to be ready. I was over the moon. To this day, I have no idea what I wore as I didn't have an evening dress in my wardrobe; I just remember that it wasn't a long gown.

As Ken and I walked down the red carpet, people in the stands were yelling with excitement, and flashbulbs were going off like crazy. Nobody knew who we were, but as we passed by, people would smile and wave, and we waved back.

"Well, Bonnie, how does it feel to be a star?" Ken asked.

We giggled as we made our way to the balcony and our seats, which were one row up from the front. We could see everything.

It was April 9, 1962. Sophia Loren was up for the Best Actress Award for her film "Two Women." The best actor Award would go to Maximilian Shell, for "Judgement at Nuremberg."

When Sophia Loren won, we stood up with the rest of the audience, cheering and clapping for her as she regally floated up to the stage as we watched from above.

We watched all the other stars as they walked around afterward, chatting and congratulating each other, the women in beautiful, beaded evening gowns, and the actors handsome in black and white tuxedoes. I pointed out stars to Ken: Natalie Wood and Paul Newman, Audrey Hepburn and Spencer Tracy, Judy Garland, and Rita Moreno.

I was in Hollywood Heaven.

Ken didn't have tickets for the after-party, but he was all for going,

"Come on, hon," he said. "What do we have to lose by trying to get in?"

Happy he wanted to take the risk, I said, "Let's go for it."

So off we went to the Beverly Wilshire Hilton, pulling in behind a line of cars waiting for the valet. We followed the other guests, hoping we could bluff our way in. I stood off to the side as Ken handed the man at the door a bill, which the man quickly stuffed into his pocket.

"C'mon, baby," Ken called to me, "We're in.

I don't know how we ever found a table with two empty seats, but we did. And we had ourselves a night to remember as we sipped champagne, ate dessert, and watched the stars mingle.

Ken and I remained friends for years and kept in touch, even if months had passed. We went to San Francisco once when he had a business appointment and wanted to see his daughter. It was a two-night trip, and we had separate rooms. He took his daughter and me to the famous Ernie's restaurant, which was elegant with beautiful, red-flocked wallpaper, dark wood furnishings, and gold-gilded mirrors and picture frames. It was all very Victorian and very Old San Francisco.

Ken was a private man, and he chose to drink to hide whatever demons chased after him. He was a buddy to whom I could open up. He'd give me advice about a guy I might be dating or something I might be worried about. I'll never know how he kept his law office going, but he managed to get along and pay his bills. He never lived a high-end life and drove the same older car as I remember.

It broke my heart years later when another lawyer friend of ours called to tell me that Ken had gone to the Veteran's Hospital in Westwood and then died a few days later. He was another one of the good guys I knew back then.

SAMMY – Continued

Sammy and I had a closeness that I would never have with another man. We were in a time and town where we both had goals, none of which were marriage. I believed we loved each other in a special way, which was really a learning lesson for me, who once believed love was for life with one man.

We would go out together as much as our schedules would allow. Our favorite places were Don the Beachcombers in Hollywood and, of course, the Naples for Italian; it was the Formosa on Melrose, across from Sam Goldwyn's Studios for Chinese, and Musso & Frank Grill on Hollywood Boulevard for steaks and chops.

We dated others from time to time. I would tell Sammy if anything was serious. I first discovered this on Sammy's end when I would come into work. The first thing I would do in the morning was make his bed and, depending on the movies and the girls in it that he'd taken to dinner, the curly black hairs and the long red hairs on the pillow always gave me the first clues.

I never said a thing. We had a silent understanding about our relationship. I knew he cared, and I accepted our relationship for what it was.

I was touched when I first received a copy of a signed life insurance policy that Sam would purchase at the airport when he traveled that left me and the kids' money if the plane crashed and he died. (In those days, these policies were always available to purchase before you flew.)

Anita, his secretary, asked me on one of our drives home whether I knew that Sam had checked into renting the house next door for me and the kids.

I told her I hadn't and changed the subject as I knew he was getting low on cash and lived from movie to movie and probably couldn't afford it. But the thought was what mattered, and life was what it was for both of us, and if he could, he probably would have given me the world. He had that kind of a heart.

Sammy would have my kids over during the summers to swim in his pool. He knew we had no air-conditioning, and those L.A. summers in our tiny dwelling were hot and miserable.

I would listen to what Sam had written after a long day at his typewriter, and I had finished dusting his book-filled shelves in his dining room, where he also kept a mannequin with medals and an Army helmet. Sam kept a large chalkboard where he would make notes about his characters for the movie he lived to write: "The Big Red

One," about his life in World War II. It would become a brilliantly told movie that was written from many layers of his heart.

I loved the way he would act things out while speaking with that big, brown Havana cigar in his mouth, the ones I would pick up for him at a specialty store in Beverly Hills. Sam was well known for his Cuban cigars at a time when we couldn't get them imported from Cuba; Sam always found a way.

When we first met, Sam was writing "Shock Corridor," the first of the two movies of his that I'd be in. My part was the first in which I'd have a few lines.

On the day of filming my scene, I overslept.

"Oh, my God, how did I do this?" I cried over and over on my hasty drive to the studio.

Near tears, I apologized to Sam for my lateness. He gave me a smile and a hug.

"Don't worry," he said. "Your scene isn't scheduled until later in the day. You would have had to sit around anyway."

It wasn't a very good start, I have to say, but I finally had that all-important first credit under my belt.

Now, I would have to join The Screen Actors Guild to do a second movie or T.V. show. I had to change my professional name from Bonnie Boyd.

So, while standing in The Screen Actors Guild office filling out the papers, I quickly came up with another name. I chose Karen Conrad, as someone once told me I looked like a Karen. I was now Karen to my Hollywood friends.

It cost more than I could afford to join SAG, but I was lucky to have met a man named Eddie Rothschild, a shy, sweet, red-headed, portly man who founded Rothschild Oil and Powerine Oil Refinery Co. in Santa Fe Springs.

Eddie, a friend and customer of Peter Fairchild, who owned Fairchild's, a well-known, posh steakhouse on La Cienega Blvd. in West LA. Peter and I had become friends when I applied for a job as a hostess. I would sometimes fill in as a hostess when someone would call in sick.

Eddie was just a nice guy with whom I'd have a drink after the dinner crowd left before I'd go home. I told him I had to join SAG, and he offered to help me.

"Sweetheart, let me have the pleasure of officially getting you started as a professional actress by paying for your SAG Membership. No strings attached," he said. "You're a sweet girl with a lot of responsibilities, and I respect you for that. I know it's not easy raising kids on your own, working and trying to break in the business."

I had to hold back my tears as he patted my hand and reached for his wallet.

"Oh, Eddie, that is so sweet of you," I said. "I will never forget you and your kindness."

Eddie gave me the money to sign with SAG, and I never have forgotten the simple thoughtfulness of this man and others in my time in Hollywood.

COLUMBIA PICTURES – HARRY COHN

One day, Sam called me to his desk where he would sit and work, usually in his shorts and a bathrobe.

"Karen, I've arranged for you to meet the head of Columbia Studios, Harry Cohn," he said. "I can't promise, but maybe something will come of it as I've put in a good word for you."

I leaned over and gave him a big hug, turning away so his big cigar wouldn't set my hair on fire. I was so excited. Hopefully, maybe this would be my big break.

On the day of my interview, I got ready in the best dress I could find, I made sure my hair and make-up were perfect, and I said my morning mantra: "I don't know what is on my way today, but it can only be good. I give thanks for all the good that I receive." Then I ran out the door and drove the Ford to Columbia Studios on Gower and Sunset.

I was scared to meet Mr. Cohn. He had a reputation for being a hardheaded dealmaker, along with being a letch.

Sammy had sent me, so maybe Mr. Cohn would be nicer to me and give me a break, even a tiny little part, or a few lines, just about anything for credit in a movie made at Columbia Pictures.

With hope in hand and a few moments of nerves. I walked into the building that I would see from across the street, the nights I would work at The Naples.

I gave my name at the guard gate and was given instructions on how to get to Mr. Cohn's office. Off I went, following his instructions until I reached the right building. After climbing a flight of stairs, I took a deep breath and opened the door to be greeted by his secretary at the reception desk. After she picked up the phone and apparently told her boss I had arrived, I was shown into Mr. Cohn's office.

The man looked small as he sat back in a leather chair behind his big dark wood desk, neatly piled with scripts and correspondence. One leg crossed over the other.

I smiled as I introduced myself.

"Thank you for seeing me, Mr. Cohn," I said.

I stood there as he looked me up and down. His eyes finally settled on my face, and after a few minutes, he scowled through his heavy eyebrows and finally replied, "Sure, Sam Fuller spoke to me about you."

He then motioned with his head for me to sit in the chair across the desk from him.

"You are a very pretty girl, but your nose is a bit too long, which would probably leave a shadow on your upper lip when filmed," I said. "I hear you have a part in Sam's new movie?"

"Yes, I do, Mr. Cohn," I said. "Sam thinks I'll do well as I'm a good actress. I've been studying with James Best, and I've done 'Little Theatre' and yes, "Shock Corridor," and…

"That's very good, dear. Well, I wish you luck, but I'd see about that nose," he said. "It was nice meeting you, Karen."

This man was dismissing me.

He knew nothing about me. He wasn't curious to find out if I could act, or to find out whether I had a few more credits, or if I could dance or sing? I was dead in the water to this old pompous jerk, no matter what.

I was stunned, speechless; I am sure I turned red. This was something new. No photographer had ever said a thing about my nose; besides, Toni Basil had wanted one like mine.

After a few minutes of staring at each other, I stood up.

"Sorry my nose is too long for you," I said. "Thank you for your time and have a good day, sir."

I picked up my wounded pride and showed my nose to the door. He had wasted my time. That was a new one and probably because I was involved with Sam.

I realized that if I was introduced by a male friend I was seeing, the guy wouldn't be up for giving me a job. They would rather give it to the girl with whom they could sleep with, even if it was a part that only had a word or two. Lesson learned!

Once home, I looked through all my photos, trying to find the shadow from my nose. I couldn't find one.

"DEB STARS" – FOREIGN PRESS CLUB 1963

SHE'LL COMPETE — One of the 18 lovely final-
ists competing for the 10 Hollywood Deb Star
crowns at the annual Deb Star Ball at the Palla-
dium Nov. 23 will be Karen Conrad, 20, of Glendora.
Miss Conrad has appeared in three motion pictures
—Shock Corridor, Twilight of Honor and The Iron
Kiss — and in television's Surfside Six and the Red
Skelton Show.

Another thing going on in Hollywood in 1963 was a
contest called the "Deb Stars," which was sponsored by the
Hollywood Foreign Press Association. Producers and
directors entered actresses into the contest, and the ten
winners for 1964 were to be chosen by private ballot by
Hollywood's Make-up Artists and Hair Stylists Guild.

I asked Sam if he would sponsor me, as a studio or producer could only enter an actress into the contest.

"Sure," Sam said. "You know I will."

It took just a letter from him and a photo for me to enter. Though I was new in town, I thought I'd give it a try.

"Who knows what might happen," I thought as I reminded myself to think positively.

I was told to show up at the first interview to meet the press members running the event. Dressed to kill and ready to put forward my best interview talents, I left with my hopes high.

Arriving at the theater, I found the other girls standing around, waiting for their turn in front of the small panel of men. We all checked each other out and said a few welcoming words to one another. I watched as the girls were called up to the table, where they would be asked about their credits and backgrounds. The men had already been sent the headshots with the sponsor letters.

My turn came toward the end of the list of girls, and I marched up to the desk smiling and feeling sure I was making a good impression on the men sitting at the table, as they all smiled and were friendly.

There had been about forty-five girls that were still in the running out of close to over a hundred, and we had been told that some would go on to the semifinals and some would be out. We would be notified who'd made the next level. Only ten would go on to be next year's up-and-coming Deb Stars.

All the girls had already gone, but I had left my jacket on a chair at the back of the stage and went back to get it.

The men were still at the table talking as a few other members joined them. They started going over pictures that one of the new men had just pulled out of his briefcase.

The new one said, "Well guys, here are the photos from the shoot we did last week with our new 1964 Deb Stars," he said. "Turned out great, don't you think?"

There were 'oohs and ahs' going back and forth between the men, along with a few names I knew: Linda Evans, Raquel, Brenda.

Faces turned around and then turned red as I stepped forward from the other side of the curtain and said, "The New Deb Stars?"

"You mean that the winning Deb Stars have already been picked? All this was just a con?" I said, feeling my anger rise. "What kind of contest is this anyway? Shame on you, putting all us girls through this and getting our hopes up for nothing."

They looked worried as one of the guys walked over to me and said, "Okay, you got us. I'm sorry, and you're right; the winners have already been picked. I am so sorry. It's too late now as all the photos have already been taken, and the press releases are already written and ready for release. It's too late to put you in the top ten, but we will at least put you in the eighteen semifinalists. It's all that can be done at this point."

I was furious.

"Forget it. This is just another con job that I won't forget!" I said as I turned with my jacket in hand and walked out.

The newspaper came out with pictures of a few of the eighteen semifinalists. My name was listed as one of the eighteen. I did find one small town paper that had an article with my name and picture that I could add to my scrapbook.

The final ten winning girls were from the big studios; of course, it was all rigged. Another dream down the drain, another lesson learned.

Sam was busy working on his next movie, "The Naked Kiss," with Michael Dante, Anthony Eisley, and Constance Towers (who was then married to Gene McGrath and later the actor John Gavin). Connie was married to Gene during the filming, and we would be invited to their beautiful mansion in Beverly Hills.

Once, Sam was invited to visit them at their second home in Panama. Sam brought back beautiful silver, woven wraps as gifts for Anita and me. Anita's was white, and mine was a glorious turquoise that made my blue eyes stand out. Sam really had a big heart and would always think of others with little surprises.

I was working part-time for Sam, which gave me more time to spend with Robin and Chris. It was difficult being their sole financial support, but I had Rita, who was always there to watch the kids and take them on annual summer trips to visit family at a ranch in Wyoming. I never asked her for any financial help from Will's family, even though her son never paid child support, and my mother and Bill never offered any help. I had made my bed, and the responsibility was mine.

LIFE BETWEEN MOVIES

Between my parts in Sam's "Shock Corridor" and "The Naked Kiss," to be filmed in 1964, I would do various other show business appearances.

I met Jayne Mansfield and Mickey Hargitay at a parade we participated in before the Ken Mile's Road Race at Dodger Stadium. Mickey invited me to be interviewed on T.V.'s "The Mickey Hargitay Show." Mickey was a hot bodybuilder and husband to Jayne Mansfield, a well-endowed, sexy, blonde actress. Their daughter Mariska Hargitay would gain fame on her own years later with her T.V. Series, "Law and Order: Special Victims Unit."

I was hired to be the girl giving the trophies on a TV bowling show and then at a few car racing events. I was awarded the title of "Miss Los Angeles Blades," touting the Los Angeles ice hockey team.

I went to events promoting movie theatre openings along with other up-and-coming actors and actresses like Barbara Eden, Telly Savalas, Norm Alden, Gary Crosby, Kevin Corrigan, Rod Taylor, Vic Morrow, Tony Bill, and Annette Funicello.

I met an up-and-coming writer named Harlan Ellison, who would become well known both for his prolific and influential work in new-wave science fiction as well as for his combative personality. We shared a dinner or two, and I had listened while he spun his wild stories. A girlfriend from Glendora had come to Hollywood to be an actress, but she had no place to go, so I gave her a place to stay on my couch. She ended up running off with Harlan two days later.

I was seen dining with Norman Alden at The Luau in Beverly Hills, Jack Kosslyn at Chez Voltaire, Andy Prime at the Villa Capri, Sam Fuller at Don the Beachcomber's, and Don Ingels at The Guys and Doll; in other words, I was getting press. Getting your name in the columns was important for a newbie.

I was asked by Johnny Grant, known as "Mr. Hollywood," to visit injured vets at the Westwood Veteran's Hospital. It was sometimes quite heartbreaking to see their faces filled with pain, despair, and depression. I would crack jokes and give them encouragement, hoping to lift their spirits as best I could. Some days, I left with a small smile, knowing I had added a little cheer to a man's life just by being there, while some days, I would leave with a lump in my throat and a tear trying to break through.

I also think it was Johnny Grant who asked me and Julie Redding, a beautiful, tall, long-haired blonde, to fly in a small plane to a prison in Tehachapi.

It would be my first time flying on a tiny airplane, and I was frightened. I hid my fear and, believe it or not, was given the controls to fly the plane by myself for a few minutes. Julie and I performed a funny little skit and got a lot of whistles and applause from the sea of inmates in the auditorium.

I also helped a few times at the Hollywood Canteen on Cahuenga Boulevard, a club that operated during the latter part of WWII and offered food, dancing, and entertainment for servicemen on their way overseas. I loved meeting people and putting smiles on their faces; sometimes, I would bring the kids and they would always be the center of attention.

I got in touch with Julie years later, in the '80s, after she had married her third husband, Hubert Hutner, the chairman of the President's Advisory Committee on the Arts from 1982-90, serving under Presidents Ronald Reagan and George H.W. Bush.

They were living in Bel Air, and I was asked if I wanted to do some part-time secretarial work for Herb. I said, "Sure," and was given an office in a tiny room with a small high window that I believed was once a closet, as there was barely room for anything but a desk, chair, and waste basket.

My job would be short-lived. Besides the day's work, I was asked to attend a large dinner party and watch the guests and kitchen staff to make sure nobody took anything. This was an impossible task as I couldn't be in two places at once.

The next day I was informed that I was let go as someone had taken a few pieces of the silver place settings.

MGM – BILL PERLBERG "TWILIGHT OF HONOR"

I don't remember how I met Bill Perlberg, a producer at MGM in Culver City, but I think it may have been through a friend who recommended me for a part in his next film.

William Perlberg, one of the well-known, high-ranking producers in town, was known for casting Grace Kelly in the hit movie "The Country Girl" in 1954.

He started in the business as an agent at William Morris and later as a talent agent and personal assistant to Harry Cohn. He went on to produce many box office hits for some of the biggest studios in town. He worked in association with George Seaton on films, including "Miracle on 34th Street" and "Chicken Every Sunday."

I remember going to his office at MGM. Standing in front of this kindly, still good-looking older man who easily could have been my grandfather, we would go through all the usual questions about my acting experience.

Then he said the magic words.

"I think I may have a small part in a new movie we are getting ready to film next month," he said. "Maybe, if the director, Boris Segal is okay with it, we can get you a bigger speaking part, but I can't promise."

"Oh, my God," I said to myself as I broke out in a big smile.

Then I found the words to say to the man.

"Thank you so very much, Mr. Perlberg," I said. "I'm so thrilled."

He beamed.

I passed all the tests and came up with a small part in his new movie, "Twilight of Honor." I would be on the set with Nick Adams, Claude Rains, Joan Blackman, James Gregory, Joey Heatherton, Linda Evans, and Richard Chamberlain. This would be Richard's first movie as he was already well known as "Dr. Kildare," playing the lead in the hit TV series.

Someone would call me with all the details. Bill Perlberg smiled at me, stood up from his desk chair, and walked me to the door.

"I'm sure you'll do well, Karen," he said warmly.

I got the call to report to the set and meet the director, Boris Segal, before filming. I was excited to watch him work with all these great actors.

This job also gave me a nice check to take home for a down payment on a place to rent. The kids and I had been invited to stay at a girlfriend's apartment until I could find someplace affordable for us to live. I had the couch and the kids slept in her son's room.

I never asked Sammy for any money. I worked for what I made and was paid hourly for the housecleaning and errands I ran.

In the movie, I was playing the girlfriend of Cole Clinton's son, played by Lee Anthony. Cole Clinton was the victim of a murder. Nick Adam's character, Ben Brown, was the accused, and he would be on trial throughout the movie. Richard Chamberlain was playing David Mitchell, Ben's lawyer.

During filming, I would spend my time sitting, observing the trial, comforting my boyfriend while waiting for the lines I hoped to speak...

One night, about a week or two after meeting with Mr. Perlberg, I received a telephone call. It was Bill Perlberg,

"Hello, Karen, how are you doing, my dear," he said. "Excited, I hope?"

"Oh yes, very excited, Mr. Perlberg," I said. "Is everything okay?"

"Oh yes," he said. "I was just thinking about you and thought of checking in to see how you're doing."

And then he asked me to have dinner with him.

I was stunned. This seemed to come out of the blue. Usually, a request for a date would come at the office after an interview, but this was different. Bill was different. And I sensed a loneliness about him as if there was something he was missing in his life. He didn't have the hardness about him that others did; he carried with him a kind of sadness.

Taken back, I thought for a minute before replying.

"Thank you, that's very sweet of you to ask, but I have two little children, and I need to arrange for a sitter," I said.

"Karen, do that," he said. "Arrange for one for Wednesday night. I'll pick you up at 7:30. I believe you are on Fountain off Gower, correct? I have your address here."

"That's correct, Mr. Perlberg," I said.

"Call me Bill," he replied. "I'll see you Wednesday, my dear."

I turned to my girlfriend and said, "I think I'm in trouble."

Right on time on Wednesday night, Bill came to the door of the small apartment where the kids and I were staying. I answered the doorbell with a smile and invited him in and introduced him first to my roommate and then to my children.

"This is Robin, who's in kindergarten now," I said. "And Chris, who is three."

Bill surprised me with his attention to the kids. Bending his knees, he got down to their level, saying, "Well, you two, looks like you're having a good time playing with those toys. Chris, let me see that truck; ah, that's a fancy one. Wish I'd had one like that when I was a kid."

Bill turned to me and said, "Karen, you sure have two beautiful kids here."

Turning back to Robin, he said, "Well, pretty girl, you take after your mother." He then put his hand out, first to Robin and then to Chris.

"Shake my hand," he said as they complied. "There you go. Time for your mother and I to go have dinner."

I grabbed my coat and purse, kissed the kids, and followed Bill to the door. He turned to the kids and my roommate.

"Goodbye. It was nice meeting you," he said. "See you kids soon."

"You're very lucky, Karen. They're sweet kids," he said while he started the car. And then off we went to have dinner at Musso & Frank in Hollywood, not far from the apartment.

We had a very nice, easy conversation over dinner, mostly talking about the film business and the new film I'd have a small part in. I didn't say anything about "having lines" or anything about my part, as I was just thrilled to be in a major picture.

Bill took me back to the apartment, walked me to the door, and kissed my cheek.

"I enjoyed our evening, Karen, and meeting the kids," he said.

I thanked him for being so sweet to them and for the wonderful dinner.

"We will have to do it again, Karen," he replied with another cheek kiss. He walked back to his car, waved, and pulled away into the night, leaving me to ask myself, "What do I do now?"

A few days later, Bill called again to ask me out to dinner, and when he arrived, he asked to come in to say hello to the kids.

We sat on the couch, and again, he took time to talk with the kids until we had to go in time for our dinner reservation at Martoni's, another restaurant not far from the apartment.

Going home that night ended up no different from the first night, but I knew that would soon change. Bill was a gentleman and a very smart man who sooner or later would let his expectations come to light, just as it had always happened before with the men in my life.

Apparently, the third time was a charm. After spending time at the apartment with the kids and me, with my roommate out of the room and Robin and Chris watching T.V., Bill put his arm around my shoulders as we sat on the couch and brought up a conversation I hadn't expected or wanted to have.

I told myself when I started this Hollywood journey that I wouldn't sleep with a man just for a part. I did not want to be like the others who did. But this was a little different.

Sammy hadn't offered me a part when we became involved, and I had quickly grown to care about the man, and I knew what the limits to our relationship would be.

Bill started off by saying, "Karen, I really do care about you. I hope you know that. I also really enjoy these times being with you and the kids.

"Thank you, Bill, I'm glad you have," I replied, wondering where all this was going.

I would soon find out and must say I was surprised as he found the words he wanted to say.

"Karen, I want you to think about something before you answer," he said. "I keep an apartment in Beverly Hills, and I would like you and the kids to move in."

I sat there, taken aback as I never expected this from this man I hardly knew. I knew what would be expected, as I was being asked to be a kept woman. This hadn't crossed my mind before, as how often does a man in his position want a woman with the baggage of two little kids when they could easily have a "hungry for a part actress" anytime they wanted!

Bill was different.

I must say I enjoyed being with him, and the idea was entertaining for a more than just a moment or two. There was Sammy, and there were my Catholic morals, and there was my financial situation, which also entered the battle that raged through my thoughts as I had found out he was married.

"Bill, isn't it time we leave for dinner?" I asked. "I'm so surprised by your kind offer, and I need time to think about this, and a stiff drink might help."

Bill looked a little surprised as he got up from the couch and nodded toward the door, turning to the kids to tell them "Goodnight" as we were leaving.

We both said little on the way to the restaurant, and we managed to get through the meal. I knew he was patiently waiting for an answer.

As we sat in his car in front of the apartment, I gave him my answer.

"Bill, I am so flattered that you care so much about the kids and me that you would offer to take care of us," I said, "but it wouldn't be fair of me to go into a relationship like this knowing that you're married and have a wife at home.

"I think a lot of you and have enjoyed every moment we have spent together, but I can't do it. I must turn your offer down. I'm sorry, Bill."

He quietly walked me to the door with what I would come to believe was a crushed ego. He bent down and kissed me on the lips, gave me a hug, looked into my eyes for a moment, and said, "Goodbye Karen, I wish you well."

I never would be given any lines during the filming, but I would go up to Boris Segal anyway and kid him, saying, "Where are my lines, Boris?" He would give me a big smile each time and shrug his shoulders, and I smiled back, and we both laughed. I'm sure he knew something had gone down between Bill and me, or should I say, "didn't go down."

Boris was a sweet man, and I would have a great time with everyone working on the set. It became like a family for those two weeks of filming as the crew and actors took me under their wings.

Red Berry would come up each morning and say hello, and we would chat about the scenes being shot that day. Jeanette Nolan would say hello and ask me how my kids were. James Gregory had a wonderful dry sense of humor, as I would find during the shoot, and Claude Rains would walk over to say hello and chat me up. I spent time getting to know Nick Adams, who had been in "Rebel Without a Cause" with James Dean and was part of that crowd. We would meet up at a party a few months later.

I would be asked by Linda Evans's agent to join them for dinner at Trader Vic's at the Beverly Hilton Hotel one night. We laughed a lot and had a wonderful Cantonese dinner, sharing ribs and egg roll appetizers before the main course. We drank fruity rum drinks with colored paper umbrellas resting on the sides of our glasses.

Richard Chamberlain would be the only one with a cool reserve, but I chalked that up at the time to the fact that this was his first movie. Years later, I understood more when I learned that he was a closeted gay man.

TIM CONSIDINE AND EARL LEAF –
PARTY TIME

It was at this time that I met "The Beatnik,"
photographer Earl Leaf, who would become a friend and
who would introduce me to the young Hollywood set that
would become a fun part of my life.

There were so many new names to remember, as Earl
always had an open door at his parties. Some names I knew
as they were popular young actors and actresses who were
always in the Hollywood gossip columns of Harrison
Carroll, Hedda Hopper, and Louella Parson, the most-

known columnists in those years; Earl wrote his "My Fair and Frantic Hollywood" column for "Teen Magazine."

Soon, my name would start appearing in Earl's columns. As the weeks passed, the others would follow, as I became known as a "budding new actress in town."

"Karen, I want you to meet someone I think you'll like," Earl said one day. "He's really one of the nice guys."

I knew his name as he was working on "My Three Sons," playing the part of Fred McMurray's oldest son, Mike.

Tim Considine was an early member of Disney's "The Mickey Mouse Club." I knew he was a well-liked, cute actor. He began his career in "The Clown" at the age of twelve, playing the part of Red Skelton's son. Tim would quit "My Three Sons" in 1964.

He would continue to act, write, and direct throughout the following years. Tim had been born into a show-business family: his father was a director, and his mother came from the Pantages Family. Sadly, I've learned Tim died in 2022 at the age of eighty-one.

Earl was having a party at his house the next night, at which I would be introduced to Tim. Earl went through some of the names on the guest list that I might know: Paul Peterson, Jill Banner, who would end up being Marlon

Brando's girlfriend, Jenny Maxwell, Ty Hardin, Cheryl Holdridge, Perry Lopez, one of the Crosby boys, Max Baer, Jr., Don Grady and a few others, whose names weren't familiar to me.

Earl didn't have a large house, so everyone hung where they could find room. Some were outside, smoking something we didn't mention at that time, although we sure could smell that pungent aroma. Earl and his home were totally what you'd expect from a fun-loving '60s hippie. He was well thought of, loved by all, and, yes, he never made a pass at me.

Paneled wood walls were filled with photos signed by the many stars he had photographed, and yes, there were a few of Marilyn Monroe. Wood furniture with well-worn couches and chairs filled the main room. A small kitchen was off the living room, as I remember, while a wooden bar separated the two rooms.

A tiny bathroom was off the living room, across from his bedroom. I will never forget that bathroom. Later, at another gathering, I had followed a few others to where they stood at the opened bathroom door, watching, giggling, and making comments about what was going on in there.

I had peeked over someone's shoulder and was completely shocked. A very well-known young actor was having sex with an unknown naked girl. Both were standing up, screwing in the shower for all to see.

"You don't need to see this," Tim said as he grabbed my hand and led me away.

This was a first for me. I was still naive about sex in public in those days, not that I would ever be into anything like swinging. I was a mother, raising kids.

A few of the couples who were dating sat on the couches or stood against the wall, the girl pinned in by the guy kissing and making his advances.

Tim, escorted by Earl who, with a sly, proud, fatherly look, introduced us.

"Tim, this is Karen Conrad," he said.

"Hello Karen," Tim said. "I'm happy I finally get to meet you."

"Same here Tim, my pleasure. I'm glad our friend Earl here loves getting people together," I said with a flirty smile, impressed with the young guy standing in front of me.

Tim was a doll, about 5 feet 9 inches tall, with big blue eyes, dark blonde hair, freckles, and the sweetest aura that made a girl feel at ease, which I did. I smiled as he took my hand and led me over to the bar where the liquor bottles were, asking what I would like.

"A glass of red sounds good," I said.

He poured a little of the red wine, probably Gallo, at that time, in one of Earl's water glasses and grabbed a beer for himself from a tub filled with ice, bottled beer, and sodas. Tim then led me out the front door to a quiet, softly lit area where a few lawn chairs sat in front of some foliage on the side of Earl's property.

We both started talking at once with questions about our present lives. Tim had been told I had two children, and he asked questions about them and seemed to enjoy my telling him about my little ones. Not all actors wanted to hear about a woman's children, as most seemed to need to be the main object of a woman's time and attention, and some felt children got in the way, which they could and did.

Tim and I really hit it off. Being the gentleman that he was, he walked me to my car.

"Karen, I really enjoyed meeting you tonight and would love to see you again," he said. "Do you mind if Earl gives me your number?"

"I would love to see you again, Tim, and yes, I'm sure Earl already has it written down, ready to give to you," I said.

We laughed as Tim opened my car door for me. Closing the door, I rolled down the window and blew him a kiss before he walked away with a smile on his face and a return kiss gesture.

Tim was in the middle of filming "My Three Sons" episodes for the season, and being on set could take up most of the day and early evening. Morning calls can be early, and you could be up at 5 a.m. and home at 7 p.m. or later if grabbing a bite to eat on the way home, or if filming ran late.

You might not be filming all day. But you mostly had to stay on the set and be ready if the director had a change of plans for a scene or you were asked to do an interview or pose for promotional photos. You were paid a flat fee to be there, not an hourly wage.

Tim called, and we got together again for a wonderful evening of dinner out, full of nice conversation, and ending with a make-out session, and then him walking me to my door with both of us wanting more but holding the passion back for the time being.

Our next date was spent at Tim's house, where I was surprised to find he had prepared a tasty Italian dinner for us. Later, with appetites sated with pasta and red wine, I followed him to his candle-lit bedroom, where we would make tender, sweet love for the first time. Then, some moments later, we would find we were still hungry for each other, and he would slowly coax me, teasing me with his searching hands, tasting me with his still-hungry lips and tongue, making my body come alive again until the passion grew between us, consuming us until it became a wild ocean wave invaded by hot, molten lava.

We continued our journey of delightful sexual adventures a few days later, again at his house.

My marriage to Will had brought two inexperienced kids together. I never knew what sex was during our years together. This was all a new thing for me, and I would open to passion. Sadly, I had not found it with Sammy. The passion I shared with him was of the mind, heart, and spirit, not the body.

I had told Sammy at this time I was dating someone, as was our silent agreement; he nodded and gave a small smile as he wanted me to live life and grow. He was wise in his thinking and age, and he knew life's moments were to be shared and not taken from the experiences of people you loved.

A month or so later, I would tell him I was engaged, and he again nodded, giving me a bit of a smile. "Well, I guess I need to say congratulations," he said.

The engagement was not to Tim, unfortunately. I will always regret that I chose to follow the moment and walk away from Tim.

JIM MITCHUM – A BUMP IN THE ROAD

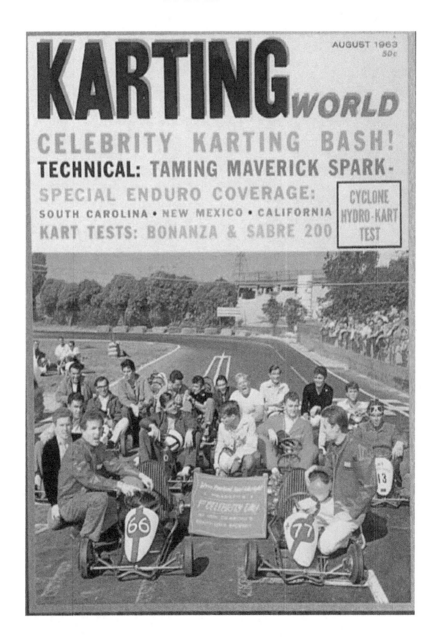

Von Deming's South Gate Raceway was hosting A Celebrity Go-Kart Cart Race on a hot, muggy Southern California day. The track was paved, yet dust would fly along with the black rubber residue from tires skidding in the turns. These Karts were not homemade: they were expensive, single-engine, modified class, factory-made Karts that would go around the track, reaching the top speed of 50 mph for the guys, which, for the celebrities, was the top speed allowed by the insurance companies. The girls were limited to a top speed of 35 mph in the single-engine stock class.

Some of the lucky drivers had sponsors. This was a serious business for these guys, and there was no turning back once they got into it. Each driver left any remnants of fear behind. They listened for the roar of the crowd; they waited for the wave of the checkered flag, and they fought to be the first to cross the finish line and claim the trophy.

This was where Tim spent most weekends, on the track that he loved for the thrill of speed and the high it gave him.

Tim and I would talk during the week, but his schedule at the studio kept us apart for a week or so after that second night of passion.

One night, I picked up the phone and smiled at the sound of Tim's voice.

"Hi Karen," he said. "Can you get a sitter for the kids for Sunday? I want to take you to the latest celebrity craze in town, or I should say out of town, as it's held at South Gate Raceway about a half hour away from Hollywood, depending upon the traffic."

I told him I'd love to go, and we made our plans. He was picking me up at 7:30 a.m.

"Are you racing," I asked.

"You bet," he said. "And you're racing, too. There's a race for the girls, Karen. It's easy and I know you can do it."

I told him I'd never driven a Go-Kart in my life.

"And you want me to enter a race in front of hundreds of people? Where I could get hurt." I protested.

"I'll give you a lesson when we get there," he said. "You'll be fine. Don't worry."

His reply calmed my fears for the moment.

On Sunday, I rolled out of bed early, got the kids fed and dressed for the babysitter, who soon knocked on my door.

"Good morning, girl," I said, chuckling as she came in.

I watched her rub the sleep from her eyes as she tried to hide a big yawn.

"Yeah, I know it's early. The kids are fed," I said as I returned to the bathroom to finish putting on my make-up.

Tim was soon knocking on the door as I finished pulling my sleeveless, pink, cotton sweater over my sandy blonde hair and pulled on my white capris. I rushed out to greet Tim and head out for my first race, or what would be a new and somewhat exciting bump in the road.

"Wow, Tim," I said as my eyes took in the crowd of people already lining up to buy tickets for the grandstand. Others were roaming around. Chatting with each other, young and old. I had no idea that this was a big thing, and I didn't expect a crowd of this size.

The fear crept in again.

"Tim, I don't know about being in this race," I said over the noise of the crowd as I tried to back out of participating. "There are a lot of people out there and I don't have a clue as to what to do. This might not be such a good idea."

"Come on, Karen, I'll show you," Tim replied as we made our way to the Kart he would drive.

Away we went, passing a guard at a separate entrance for the drivers and crews and the photographers who would be running all over the place, trying to get their shots of the young stars-to-be and the well-known, older stars who were hardcore racers.

Some of the racers that day: Kennan Wynn, Bruce Kessler, Von Deming, Budd Albright, James Mitchum, Steve Rowland, Paul Peterson, Les Brown Jr., Michael Landon, Troy Donahue, Telly Savalas, Tuesday Weld, Stephanie Power, James Drury, Nick Adams, Don Grady, Mickey Callan, Linda Evans, Chad Everett, Robert Fuller, Connie Stevens, Jay North, Pernell Roberts, Tommy Kirk, Jenny Maxwell, Fabian, Max Baer Jr., and the list goes on and on.

It was to be a day of "Male Hunks and Beautiful Starlets" all on display, ready to race and have their pictures taken, and I was one of them. It would be a day of the bad boys on the make for any new face that would catch their eye, including me, on this day of dust and the mixed roar of engines and cheers. It was to be a day of new beginnings.

When we got to the Kart, Tim had me watch as he started the engine, turned the wheel, drove a few feet, and showed me how to brake.

"Ok, Karen, let's go over to the Kart you're going drive," he said as he led me to another one." This is it; take a seat and let's see how you do. Come on, girl, it's easy."

Following his instructions, I slid into the Kart. Pushing the starter button, then the gas pedal, off I went with a few starts and stops until I got the hang of it.

"That was great, Karen," Tim said happily. "I knew you could do it!"

I was getting my confidence up enough to feel I might get through the day.

"Tim," I said, "this really is fun."

***

"Ladies and Gentlemen, the men's race will begin," the announcer called into the microphone. "Good luck to all"

Engines roared and helmets went on. I quickly bent down, kissed Tim's cheek, said, "Go get them, honey," and away he went.

I watched these guys go round and round the track with speeds soon reaching the limit of 50 mph. Bumping into each other, cutting each other off, some sliding off the track and making it back on again, rubber burning, they were doing everything possible to stay on that track to reach the finish line and the checkered flag. Some drivers got run off the track, their engines sputtering out. Some threw up their hands when their Karts wouldn't start again. Some walked away mad. And some held on until the end.

The roar of the crowd grew as the final drivers made their way to the finish line. Cheer from the grandstands grew as Tim made it across the finish line and the checkered flag dropped. Tim won first place.

He climbed out of the Kart, turned to the crowd, waving until he turned to where I was standing, smiling. I gave him a thumbs-up as he walked over to me.

"I did it, I won!" he said.

He was a sight to see. His big, happy smile made thin brown lines because of the dust and black tire residue that still clung to his face; some of it settled in at the bottom of his cheeks as his smile grew, and some lay in the laugh lines at the ends of his bright, shining blue eyes. I gave him a big hug and kiss, and all the others crowded around to congratulate him.

It was my turn next as they announced the girl's race. Still warm and happy from the glow of Tim's win, my helmet went on, and again, I slid down into the low seat, legs straight out, hands on the wheel. With my heart in my throat, I pushed the starter button, revved the engine of the Kart, and, with all the other girls, listened for the announcer's words, "Get ready!" as the green flag dropped.

Off I went on the dusty track, with its turns and straightaways, with about thirty or so other girls helmeted in their small Karts.

Some would bump and sway and run off the road, and then sit there trying to start their Karts back up. I continued with the dust constantly coming at me; with my heart pounding, I hung in, and round after round I went.

The group of girls was now down to about twelve, and I was stuck at the end of the group as we approached the last turn. All of a sudden, the Karts ahead of me started crashing into each other, one after another, apparently after the lead driver got hit and spun around. I couldn't believe my eyes as they just sat there stunned. I quickly decided I would just go around them.

I pushed down on the pedal and took off, driving as fast as I could before someone decided to get out of the group and come racing after me. I couldn't believe it, as no one did, and I crossed the finish line, the checkered flag dropped, and I won the race. Pretty good for a first-time driver! I almost cried with joy and pride as Tim came running over and grabbed me as I climbed out of the Kart and into his arms.

After all the congratulations, photo shoots, driving home, and cleaning ourselves up at my house, I picked up my car and followed Tim to celebrate our wins with the Kart crowd at The Villa Capri in Hollywood.

Drinks flowed, and music played, but it was barely audible with the back-and-forth shouting and laughter. The celebration was in high gear by the time we arrived.

"Karen, come over here I want you to meet a friend of mine who's going to entertain us tonight with a few songs," said my buddy Earl Leaf. In front of me stood Kitty Jones, a beautiful, blonde, full-figured woman with a Kim Novak face and smiling blue eyes.

"Well, hello, Karen," Kitty said as she turned to Earl. "You were right on, Earl, she's a looker."

That night Kitty and I became friends for life.

Kitty was from Texas and full of life. She welcomed everyone, knew everyone, made friends, made introductions. I would meet many people in the movie business during my years knowing Kitty, like Clint Eastwood, Elvis Presley, Hugh O'Brien, Norman Alden, Jason Evers, Trini Lopez, Cathy Crosby, Anna Capri, Rosemary Forsyth, Henry Jones, Ty Hardin, the Crosby Boys, as well as the attorney Arthur Crowley, a prominent Beverly Hills lawyer.

You name them, and she knew them. Some of the guys I would date, and some I would hang out with at Kitty's. She was a real Hollywood Godmother.

I would later date Hugh O'Brien, who starred as Wyatt Earp in the popular T.V. series, after we met at a party at Kitty's. Hugh took me to the Playboy Mansion, and we'd go to Laker's basketball games, where we would sit in the private box of Jerry Buss, who owned the team. Hugh took me to meet his brother and sister-in-law in Long Beach, and I really liked being with him until the first night he took me to his house off Mulholland Drive and Coldwater Canyon for the first time that we would make love.

We were just getting to the point of intimacy after making out on his bed when I heard a loud, scary scream from a woman a short distance away. It scared the hell out of me, and I jumped up.

"What was that? Hugh, someone needs help. We need to call the police or go outside and find out what's happening," I said. "Hugh, get up. Aren't you going to do something?"

I heard another high-pitched scream coming from somewhere nearby. I then said to Hugh, "She could be hurt and needs help."

He just looked up at me and said, "Don't worry, she lives in my guest house down the hill and she's OK."

Well, that was the end of that romantic moment, and although I really liked the guy (he once complimented me on my "beautiful, childbearing hips." How many men would say that?), I didn't date him again after that. He was just another lesson in life.

Kitty worked during the day at an office and later would open her own employment business in Woodland Hills, where she moved after marrying one of Clint Eastwood's stuntmen, Richard Lee. When I first met Kitty, she would sing at some of the smaller, intimate clubs in Hollywood at night. We would all go to a party and give her our support. She wasn't the greatest singer, but she was a fun, well-loved entertainer.

Steve Rowland, Kitty Jones & Budd Albright

The other female friend I made that night was a darling, Norwegian blonde actress named Jenny Maxwell, who played the part of the spoiled blonde girl Elvis turned over his knee and spanked in the movie, "Blue Hawaii." We both had young children and we became friends quickly.

Tim had been busy talking to friends as I chatted with Kitty, Earl, and Jenny. I said to the group, "I'll be back in a few minutes. Let me grab a drink for Tim and me." I headed over to the bar and was blocked by the big, tall, dark-haired, grinning actor, Max Baer Jr., who played the part of Jethro Bodine on the "Beverly Hillbillies," hit T.V. series.

Max, with his full, smiling face (and who was probably half-lit by then), said, "Hey, pretty girl, I've been trying to talk to you all day, but you haven't given me the time of day. What's up with that?"

Yep, Max had been chasing me all day and I had been doing everything to be polite and unavailable. I was with Tim and not interested in meeting him.

"Max, I'm sure you're a nice guy, but I'm busy with the one I'm with at the moment. I am not interested, Max."

Max looked like I had deflated his ego, but he tried again.

"Oh, come on, Karen, give a guy a chance," he said, slurring his words a bit.

"Bye, Max, Tim is waiting for his drink," I said as I moved to get around him and through the crowded bar. I left Max standing there, taking another slug of his drink to help him through his defeat.

I finally got the drinks and made my way through the crowd to Tim.

"Hey, I thought you might need this by now," I said as I handed him his drink and placed a kiss on his cheek.

"Thanks, hon, but after this I better get home," he said. "Tomorrow is Monday and I have a very early call. Good thing we stopped and got your car on the way so you can hang out a little longer. I know you want to hear Kitty sing. I'll give you a call during the week."

Then, he said he was proud of me winning the race. "I knew you could do it,"

He looked worn out from the long day in the hot sun, and I knew he was beat.

"We both came out winners today," I said. "You were a great teacher. Get some sleep, and we'll talk soon."

We kissed, hugged and I watched him leave, not aware of the four guys standing in a group in the corner, also watching him leave me standing there alone.

I should have left when he did, but I was on a high after a wonderful day, and I was thrilled to make a few new girlfriends to hang out with; the ones I'd met on the strip were nice but lived in a different world of men and money, and I'm sure the only acting they did was in the bedroom.

I heard the music stop, and I knew it was time for Kitty to sing. Up she came with her microphone and stood under a lighted area. The crowd gathered around as she greeted everyone.

"Wow, what a day this has been," she said. "I know you all are tired after this long, exciting day out in the heat, so I'll try to keep the songs cool for you, but let's start off with a kind of warm one."

She launched into one of the group's apparent favorites, "A Good Man is Hard to Find," but changed the words to "A Hard Man is Good to Find." She sang, and everyone applauded and laughed, nudging each other now and then.

Kitty knew her audience, and she had fun with them. Halfway through her set, I felt someone come up and stand close behind me. Turning around suddenly, I looked up to see this young, handsome guy looking down at me with a sly smile on his face.

Jim Mitchum. I remembered seeing him a few times at the race, glancing over to Tim and me. I also watched him on the racetrack, driving at such high speeds and taking tons of risks that I had been sure he'd crash. But he didn't. He was very skilled at what he was doing.

He smiled and introduced himself.

"I'm Jim," he said, "and I heard you're Karen."

"It's nice to meet you, Jim," I said. "I saw you race today. You're quite a driver. I had to catch my breath a few times when you came close to losing it, but you really hung on those turns."

Jim laughed.

"I've had a lot of experience," he said.

Yep, I bet he had in more ways than one, I thought to myself.

Jim was charming, with a little bit of a 'boyishness' about him that could quickly get to a woman's heart if she let it; I'm afraid I did.

Jim's friend, Budd Albright, came over to say something to Jim about leaving. Jim said to wait a bit as he wanted to get to know me. Budd got the hint and walked away to talk to their friend Steve Rowland, standing by the bar.

Kitty had finished her set, and Jim and I turned around to applaud as she made her way to us.

"Well, there's tall, dark, and handsome, and my new friend, Karen," she said, laughing. "Better watch this guy, Karen. He's lethal. I'm warning you, girl."

"You know I'm just kidding, Jim," she said to him.

And then she turned to me and gave me a wink that backed up what she had said: "Watch this guy."

"So, Tim had to leave? Not such a good idea to leave a pretty girl alone," Jim said. "I'd like to get to know you better, Karen."

"I was going to leave after Kitty finished her set, but I could wait a few minutes longer." I replied.

With a big grin, Jim took my hand. "Come on, let's sit at that table over there for a few minutes."

We sat and talked longer than a few minutes. I'm sure he walked me to my car. I don't remember what all was said, but Jim was sweet and knew the right words to say to convince me to give him my number.

He called the next day and every day after. He did a good job of sweeping me off my feet. He was well-versed in the art of seduction. I was flattered and I really enjoyed our conversations. Jim would also ask about the kids, which always pulls at a woman's heartstrings.

I hadn't heard a word from Tim. He hadn't called like he said he would, which was strange, but thinking back, he wasn't one to call daily like Jim. Tim was working, and Jim wasn't, and I was really finding Jimmy flattering, fun, and someone to talk to in the meantime.

It would be over a week or so before I would say "yes "to Jim's date request. One of my favorite places to go for dinner and drinks was Steve Crane's The Luau on Rodeo Drive. It was also one of Jim's.

Steve Crane was an actor/turned restaurateur who had been married to Lana Turner and fathered her daughter Cheryl Crane, who would later be charged in the death of her mother's boyfriend, Johnny Stompanato, in 1958. The killing was deemed a justifiable homicide.

The Luau was a popular Polynesian celebrity spot known for its high-profile customers. Its tiki surroundings, in cool shades of green, white, soft golds, and tans, with lattice work showing behind the palm trees and green foliage, quickly took us away from the busy, lighted evening streets of Rodeo Drive. We would be seated at a rattan, glass-top table with fan-shaped, high-backed rattan chairs made for a get-away atmosphere. We would sink into cushions soft enough to keep us in comfort for hours while sipping fruity, rum-based cocktails and nibbling on egg rolls and sticky, sweet ribs. It was the place to be in that Hollywood era.

In the days to come, our relationship grew from friends to lovers. While the kids were with the sitter, we drove up Laurel Canyon to Jim's rented house on Lookout Mountain, where we would make love until I had to get home to the kids. Jim was an experienced lover, and we were spending more and more time together.

We would meet up with his friend James Drury, who was filming "The Virginians," and his wife-to-be, actress Phyllis Mitchell, to take in dinner and a movie. The first movie was "Dr. Strangelove" directed by Stanley Kubrick, with Peter Sellers, George C. Scott, Sterling Hayden, and Keenan Wynn.

I still hadn't heard from Tim, and I knew I needed to get in touch with him and tell him about Jim before he heard it from the press.

James and Phyllis invited Jim and me to the premiere of the new, highly publicized, long-awaited movie "Cleopatra," the 20th Century Fox Studio major movie starring Elizabeth Taylor and Richard Burton. It was the major epic movie of 1963.

I was excited and, of course, did not own a long, formal dress. My mother offered to make one for me. I went to the premiere in a long, form-fitting, sleeveless, Audrey Hepburn-style, high boatneck dress. She chose a beautiful coral, iridescent, sheer fabric lined with a matching-colored satin. It was simple but elegant.

Months later, I would be hanging out with a friend, Patrick Curtis, who was taking a few headshots of me when he asked whether I had a long, formal dress that his girlfriend could borrow for an event they were attending.

"She doesn't have anything long to wear," he said.

I sent my coral, homemade dress off with him for her to try on. My dress didn't fit Raquel Welch's curvy figure, and Patrick brought it back. Raquel Welch would later become his wife. Apparently, Raquel, who had two children also, was in the same financial position as I was at that time.

The night of the premiere came, and I was nervous as could be, trying to look as glamorous as I could so Jim would be proud of being seen with a girl in a homemade dress on a night as big as this one.

It was a night I will never forget. Jim appeared at my door, handsome as ever in his black tux. He smiled and looked pleased as he complimented me.

"Karen, you look beautiful," he said. "I love the dress."

I'm sure I blushed and held back a smile at the dress remark. He held his arm out to escort me to the black limo waiting outside the run-down, white-painted back rental I lived in. That night, I was Cinderella.

The driver got out and opened the door for Jim and me, and we climbed into the dark leather interior and greeted

James and Phyllis, a very handsome couple, beautifully dressed and ready to walk down the red carpet as I was again that night.

Premiere

The spotlights were ablaze and moving around, lighting up the entire area in front of the Pantages Theatre.

The limousines lined Hollywood Boulevard to Vine Street. We waited in line and finally pulled up to the curb where the doors were opened for us; we stepped out into the glare of popping flash bulbs and the cheering crowd in the stands lining each side of the red-carpet area.

So many big stars were there that evening that I couldn't even begin to name them all. So many beautiful women in expensive gowns and jeweled to the hilt, with handsome actors or escorts walking beside them. All of Hollywood was out. Jim was giving me a night that I wouldn't forget.

James and Phyllis were stopped and led to the announcer on the sideline doing interviews, while the photographer went to town taking pictures.

Jim and I were next. Jim had recently finished his newest movie, "The Victors," with Vince Edwards. I had just finished "Twilight of Honor." This would be my first premiere interview and, somehow, my words came out with ease.

We made our way through other celebrities, who were either on their way into the theater or waiting around for their time at the microphone. Jim led me into the lobby as the four of us entered the partly darkened, ornate red-and-gilt theatre and moved down the aisle to our seats, which were midway down on the right. People greeted each other and heads turned left and right, looking for a glance at the newest celebrity to enter. Richard Burton was filming "Becket" in London at the time of the premiere and wouldn't be attending. I believe Liz was still at his side.

The theatre was full as the sound of voices dimmed along with the lights and "Cleopatra" began.

I was taken back to Egypt as the saga unfolded with the two real-life lovers, still married to others, played out their love scenes in a very believable manner. I couldn't keep my eyes off the wonderful costumes, jewelry, and the splendid opulence of the time.

This $31.1-million movie would give Walter Wagner a Best Picture Award nomination, along with Rex Harrison, who was nominated for Best Actor in a Leading Role. The only winner to take home an Oscar from the movie would be Irene Sharaff and her team for her beautiful costumes.

The movie turned out not to be the big box office success they had hoped for, but it certainly received a lot of attention and publicity with the help of Liz and Dick's flaming romance, which ended in two divorces and Liz marrying and divorcing Burton twice. Theirs was a love-filled, turbulent relationship that lasted a lifetime.

Jim and I had a wonderful time at the premiere, but by the end of the night, we were worn out from all the excitement. I was ready for the limo to head for my house to drop me off, as I was just a few miles away from the theater.

Again, the driver got out and opened the car door for Jim and me. I said goodnight and thanked James and Phyllis for sharing a wonderful evening; then Jim walked me to my door, took me in his arms, and kissed me goodnight.

All of a sudden, he explained, "Oh, my God. I think they might have left and forgotten that I left my car at their place."

Jim ran down the street to catch up with the limo, hoping they would be stopped at the corner stop sign. Apparently, they were, as I never heard differently.

I believe it was a night or two later, after going out for dinner and drinks and probably going back to Jim's to make love, that Jim brought up marriage and proposed.

What brought this on?

I'll never really know as it was so sudden, and neither of us were in any place in our lives to even go there. We were kind of into the "I really like you" stage, but it was way too soon. I've always felt Jim wanted to please his father, who wanted him to get serious and settle down and stop being a playboy.

Jim was only about twenty-three, still a young guy. Really, the idea of marriage to a girl with two small children wasn't the best idea for my unemployed actor boyfriend, or me for that matter, though I did say yes.

Jim drove me home later that night, and I was so tired all I could do was fall into bed and go to sleep.

The phone would wake me up the next morning, and it was Jim. "Hello, honey, did you tell anyone about us getting married?"

"God No, Jim, I went right to bed, and you just woke me up. I haven't had a chance to talk to anyone. Why, what's up?" I asked as I was slowly waking up.

"It's all over the news," he replied.

"Jim, did you tell anyone?"

"No," he replied, but he must have. Maybe he had too much to drink and told a friend?

The news was out, and I got a call from Harrison Carroll and a few other columnists asking for comments about our engagement. I hadn't wanted this to happen, as I had wanted to tell Tim the news before he heard it from someone else, especially through the press.

Then Tim called.

"Karen, I can't believe this," he said. "What happened, Karen? I know I haven't called for a while, but I've been busy shooting and hadn't had the time, and I just thought you knew how I felt. I guess I just took it for granted that you knew I cared for you."

I told him how sorry I was for him finding out the way he did, as I hoped to call him before the news got out, and that I had no idea how it got out so quickly.

He sounded so sad, and I felt guilty as hell for any hurt I had caused him, for he was one of the nicest stand-up guys my age that I would meet while in Hollywood. He was the type I would have been happy with instead of the bad boys I found myself choosing. I guess we must sometimes go through those to see what we really want and need.

The next night at the Luau, friends came up to congratulate Jim and me on our impending marriage. Jim was asked when he would get a ring for my finger as it was bare. None of this had been planned.

Jim had called his mother in England, and he seemed pleased to tell me that she said, "I'm so happy for you and so glad you are going to settle down now." I had called my mother, and she and Bill invited Jim and me out to dinner that weekend to celebrate.

We drove out to Glendora in Jim's orange Corvette, which I'm sure was noticed as we drove to my old house. My mother and Bill took us to the best steakhouse in town, and we celebrated with cocktails, appetizers, and the restaurant's famed corn fritters and steaks. Jim was sweet, answering all their questions about any plans, even though, at that time, we had none. We enjoyed the evening, and Jim seemed to have a good time.

The kids were excited, and Jim was good when he was with them, but it all was too soon. It was not meant to last, and it didn't.

Looking back, I think the first hint I had was a few days later when Jim came over, and after a hug, he said, "My dad (Robert Mitchum) hasn't called me to congratulate me."

I saw such sadness in him. It broke my heart as I realized how important his dad's approval was to him at that point in his young life. I think Jim had been trying to please his father with this marriage thing. It had all happened so quickly and without any forethought.

Jim had that wounded child aura at times and a sensitive inward side that showed the promise of a man with wisdom.

Once, he looked at me and said, "You know, Karen, you have the kind of face that will look just as beautiful the older you get."

It struck me how a twenty-three-year-old would think to say something like that, but Jimmy was a complex guy. He had this very sweet side that would come out of the blue at times, along with a cold word or two that could slice through your heart when you least expected it.

It might have been Carroll Righter, considered the Astrologer to the stars, who was instrumental in the end of our relationship. He was a longtime friend of Jim's and was going over our birthdates and putting together our astrology charts. He finished and looked up at us both and explained that Jim's birth sign was Taurus and mine was Libra, which was something we already knew.

We waited for him to speak again. I was hoping he would say we were a match made in heaven, but instead, we were hearing that we were not. My heart sank even lower.

"You would probably end up killing each other if you stay together," he said.

Jim and I looked at each other with shock. I remember that we didn't stay long after hearing that, nor did we say much to each other on the way back to my house. Jim dropped me off as our minds worked overtime with the man's fatal warning, which could have been the final kibosh to our relationship.

We called the marriage off, and the reporters went crazy again, this time with stories about our quick romance and break-up. There were no hard feelings between us, and my feet landed quickly on the ground as I began new chapters in my Hollywood life.

Jim and I remained friends as such. A few weeks later, he would call late one night and ask me to come up to his house, saying he was lonely. I refused. Soon, Jim would be on to the next starlet.

LIFE GOES ON – VIC MORROW

Through Jim, I met a few other friends: Budd Albright, Fletcher Fisk and his wife, and Steve Rowland, who, by this time, had left for England. Steve and I would write to each other months later after he got my address from Jim, as he was involved in the music business, and I would later become a songwriter.

Fletcher had worked with Vic Morrow, the star of the T.V. hit series "Combat." Fletcher called one day in the weeks after Jim and I parted ways and asked if I would do him a favor. His friend, Vic Morrow, needed a date for a

Director's Guild dinner. Vic had recently separated from his wife and needed a date with someone new so his wife wouldn't get any idea that he might have been involved with someone before their breakup.

I asked Fletcher what he was like.

"Vic's a cool guy," Fletcher said. "Sometimes he's a little 'out there,' but he's cool," I told him I was ready to get out there again after Jim but that there would be no funny business.

I gave him my address to give to Vic and got the date, time, and dress details. As usual, I had to figure out what to wear as this was a semi-formal affair.

When the night of this blind date came, I was dressed, made up, and a little apprehensive about meeting Vic, as I didn't know what to expect. I had later asked around and heard a few stories about his crazy sex and drug parties and something about dressing up as nuns. This I could handle as it was only a public dinner; that was the deal I made, and nothing more was to be expected. Vic was running late when he picked me up in his car for the dinner. He seemed okay but hurried, worried, and all over the place as he drove like Mr. Toad and his Wild Ride.

Vic looked up and down at his rear-view mirror, then turned his head to see the side-view mirror. He sharply turned corners, always looking behind him as though he were being chased. He drove around a block every now and then, taking us out of the way of the route to the dinner.

"She's having me followed, I just know it," he said in a raised voice. "She has a private detective after me. I know it; she's out to get me."

On and on he went until we finally, safely, arrived at the event.

I only recall a little of the conversations at the dinner. I don't remember it as an enjoyable evening as far as conversations with Vic. I was glad there were people to talk to as we sat at a round table with others.

I excused myself after dinner and made my way to the lady's room to freshen up and get a break from Vic. I was stopped by a man who rushed up to me, saying, "Angie, Angie, how are you? I had to come over and say hello when I saw you walk by."

I turned and looked up into the eyes of a handsome, older man with a smile on his face and a twinkle in his eyes. Gene Kelly, who was still smiling, said, "Oh, I'm so sorry. I thought you were Angie, Angie Dickinson. Wow, you're just as pretty and certainly do resemble her."

I introduced myself, and he took my hand and apologized once more. "It was nice meeting you, Karen," he said.

He gave me a hug before he returned to his table. I smiled, thinking that at least I had a fun moment after all the drama I was going through with Vic.

It was all I could do to get back into Vic's car as we left the venue. I couldn't wait to get out of his car after the repeat of the first ride on the return trip home, along with his rants, much louder after more than a few drinks at dinner. I don't know if it was partly due to drugs or what, but it wasn't my best memory of a Hollywood blind date.

Jim's other friend, Forrest "Budd' Albright, was a handsome, talented, charming actor, race car driver, and writer all rolled into one hunk of a man. Budd was easy to talk to and had a way about him that gave a woman a feeling of trustworthiness, which wasn't a common trait with a lot of self-absorbed actors in that town.

I always remembered the times I spent sitting in a booth across the table from Budd, discussing Hollywood, heartaches, and happiness at the famous Schwab's Pharmacy, where Lana Turner was said to have been discovered while sitting at the soda fountain. Schwab's was located at the corner of Hollywood and Crescent

Heights/Laurel Canyon during its heydays from the 1930s
to the 1950s.

***

Sam's old Ford, which I had still been driving, came to a
sad demise and had to be put out to pasture. It happened
after the kids and I were driving down the freeway for a
day at the beach when the hood of the Ford flew up into the
windshield with a sudden crash that scared the dickens out
of the kids and me, bringing us to a sudden stop at the
backend of another car.

I'll never know how I was ever able to pull over to the
side without getting hit. We made it and somehow got
towed back. We were stranded for a few weeks without a
car until Budd said he was putting his up for sale.

Budd came by the house with my used, new-to-me
yellow Chevrolet Corvair, a car they stopped producing in
1969. With Robin and Chris in the car, we proceeded to
drive up the mountains to Running Springs, where we
would pick up the car Budd would drive home.

I would meet his attractive, sweet mother, who had a
small gift shop in the little pine tree-surrounded mountain
village. The fresh air was a nice relief after the hot, smoggy

August summer in L.A. that had yet to cool down. The kids and I would have a hard time leaving the clear, cool air and blue skies, but we had to drive the car back to Hollywood before it got dark.

Budd and I spent more time than just chatting a few nights after that, though we would lose track of each other until years later when we would touch base again. He kindly lent his expert words to help me through writing this book and bring the "technical" knowledge to the Kart Chapter.

Budd would also catch me up on his life after we lost touch. Apparently, Jim Drury had asked Budd if he wanted to go on tour with the stage play, "Bye, Bye Birdie," playing Conrad Birdie (the Elvis Character). He jumped at the chance, and after his last show in North Carolina, he went to New York, where he stayed for a year before returning to Los Angeles.

I do not remember much about these chance encounters, but I had been at P. J.'s with some friends, and we had all been partying and drinking a lot that night; it was the first night out after the breakup with Jim. We were talking to some people at the table next to us, and we all decided to go to Gazarri's, which was down the street on La Cienega.

I had been talking to a guy a few years older than me with a sweet face and a pleasant smile. He was down-to-earth and had something to do with fashion and costuming, which was an interesting subject. We all ended up at his place somewhere above the strip, best I remember. We all had too much to drink, and soon it hit me.

My new friend, whose name was Bob, said he was going through a divorce, and I was going through a breakup, so it was a night to swap stories. We may have kissed a bit, but then he said, "Come on, Karen, you'll have to sleep in my bed as you can't drive after this much booze."

I knew he was right, and I didn't have to worry about him getting fresh, as he had laid down and passed out. No funny business went on that night with our inebriated conditions.

Spending the night with anyone was something I wouldn't normally do, but I knew I couldn't drive, and the kids were safe at the sitter's house on an overnight visit. In the morning, he fixed coffee and sent me on my way.

It would hit me later, when he became famous, that the Bob I'd spent the night with, was Bob Mackie, the famous fashion designer who was gay. It all made sense as to why he hadn't been all over me. I was still naïve in some ways at that time.

MALIBU PARTY – JENNY MAXWELL, NICK ADAMS, JIMMY HARRIS, MARK RYDELL, BURT SUGARMAN

Jenny Maxwell

Jenny Maxwell and I quickly became friends. We both had boys the same age who had fun playing together along with 'big sister' Robin. We would get to her house by driving up Laurel Canyon and turning on Lookout Mountain to her street.

Her mother, Anne, lived with her and always answered the door with a warm smile, greeting us with her Scandinavian accent and bending over to give each of my kids a big hug.

We would sometimes smell cinnamon when we entered the house, and we knew that soon she would bring out her warm, freshly baked cookies with glasses of cold milk for the kids.

Jenny's son, Brian, would run out, anxious to play, and Jenny and I would have coffee or, later in the afternoon, a glass of red wine. We'd share our latest dating news and gossip as we hung out in her airy, cream-colored living room.

Jenny had been dating an actor, Jack Wrather Jr., since her divorce from her ex, Paul Rapp. Paul married Jenny when she was only sixteen and new to this country after leaving Norway for New York and then moving to California to advance her acting career. Her father stayed in New York, working to keep his wife and daughter afloat in California.

Jenny had lost full custody of her son, Brian, and only had him part-time. It broke her heart. She was in the process of trying to gain full custody again, but it would be a tough battle.

Paul Rapp came from a well-to-do Beverly Hills family with a brother who was a well-known screenwriter. They had the money to pay Paul's attorney's fees and apparently, according to Jenny, to send Paul to school to study child psychology in the hopes of keeping Brian with him.

Jenny had just finished a part in Elvis Presley's new movie, "Blue Hawaii," and was on a high. We would go shopping, or Jenny went shopping, and I tagged along, as her expensive tastes took her to the high-end shops on Sunset or Rodeo Drive in Beverly Hills, where I would look with longing eyes at the beautiful fashions.

Jenny had wonderful taste in clothing and furnishings. She usually wore camels and beiges, which went well with her Nordic coloring. My shopping for clothes was at J.C. Penney's during those lean years. But I loved being with Jenny and living vicariously through her. She had a wonderful sense of humor and a flirtatious manner that I, at times, envied as I felt shy alongside her.

Jenny had invited me to a party given by Jimmy B. Harris, who had worked with Stanley Kubrick on many hit projects, including the latest hit, "Lolita."

She picked me up at my house in Hollywood in her white '58 Ford T-Bird. The party was at Harris's home in Malibu. Traffic on Highway 1 was as busy as ever on that

Sunday; the weekends during the summer months were always a nightmare if you wanted a day at the beach. We chatted about who might be there, and Jenny said something about the possibility of her boyfriend Jack showing up.

The house was beautiful and open, with walls and furnishing in modern light colors and glass. It was located on the beach, with stunning views as the sunset cast an orange glow on the sparkling, blue-grey water. People were mingling and chatting with drinks in their hands and smiles on their faces. Happy hour appetizers and drinks were passed around on silver trays by the staff employed for the party.

Jenny and I were drinking champagne when Nick Adams came over to say hello. I had met Nick on the set while filming "Twilight of Honor," and Jenny had known Nick for a while. We caught up on each other's lives since the filming.

Jenny and I were saddened and surprised when Nick explained that his wife, Carol Nugent Adams, wanted a divorce.

"She wants to take the kids and I can't lose them," Nick said, almost in tears.

He was so distressed, and Jenny and I felt so badly for him, probably Jenny even more so as she was fighting her own custody battle with Paul Rapp.

We spent another 20 minutes or so talking about Nick's situation, and at the end of our discussion, Nick asked me to have dinner with him one night the next week.

"I'm going to Hawaii at the end of the month, and I'd love to get together with you before I leave," he said.

I told him I'd love to as I looked in my purse for a pen and paper on which to write my phone number.

Nick smiled as I handed my number to him.

"I'm looking forward to it, Karen," he said, and, turning to Jenny, he said he'd be in touch.

"It was great seeing you both," he said.

As he walked away, Jenny and I both commiserated over Nick's situation with his wife. He was a very nice guy, and he loved his kids more than anything.

Jack had shown up at the party, and Jenny and I went over to say hello. On the way over to where Jack was standing talking to friends, a man stopped me and introduced himself.

His name was Mark Rydell, an up-and-coming actor, director, and producer who, at that time, was working on "Ben Casey," starring Vince Edwards. I had met Vince along with Sherry Nelson, his girlfriend at the time, and we had all hung out at Kitty's house a few times. Vince was also a big spender when it came to betting at the racetracks in southern California.

Mark would go on to be nominated for an Academy Award for directing "On Golden Pond," starring Jane and Henry Fonda. He also received Academy Award-nominations for films Including "The Fox," "Cinderella Liberty," "The River," and "The Reivers" along with "The Rose." We talked about the business and the difficulties of getting parts. It was a nice conversation. Before he left to talk to another partygoer who was waving and motioning him over, he asked for my agent's name. I took a card from my purse and handed it to him.

"It's been a pleasure talking to you, Mark," I said.

"The pleasure's mine, Karen," he replied.

I got a call from "Ben Casey" productions and was given a few lines as a nurse in an episode, "A Falcon's Eye, A Lion's Heart and a Girl's Hand," written by Barry Oranger, directed by Mark Rydell and with Harry Guardino as the guest star. I had fun and enjoyed the shoot in my nurse's uniform. Mark was a total gentleman. (I would soon wear another nurse's uniform in Sammy's next film, "The Naked Kiss.")

I also met Burt Sugarman that night. He was a well thought of man about town and a producer, best known for later creating and producing the iconic '70s to early '80s show," The Midnight Special." Burt would end up married to Mary Hart, a popular TV spokesperson who gained fame on "Entertainment Tonight."

Burt was friends with Jack and Jenny and had come over to say hello to us at the party. Burt and I struck up a conversation and were soon chatting like old friends. Jack wanted Jenny to follow him to his house, but that meant I would need a ride. Burt offered to take me home, and I took him up on it as I knew Jenny wanted a night with Jack, and she had to be careful because of the custody battle.

Burt asked if I wanted to see his new house on Mulholland Drive above the Hollywood Hills, which was really on the way with a slight detour.

The man had a solid reputation, and I wasn't worried about being alone with him. Besides, Jenny and Jack were friends, and Jenny had given me the heads-up sign after his suggestion. Besides, I figured he wanted to help them have some alone time together.

Burt's house was beautiful, as expected, perched on a hill with a full view of the lighted San Fernando Valley below. Burt brought me a glass of wine, and we sat talking on the outdoor patio, enjoying the view, until I said I needed to get home to the sitter and kids. Burt took me home and walked me to the door, and I thanked him for the ride. We said goodnight, and that was that. I appreciated not having to worry about turning someone down; it was nice and easy, and he was a perfect gentleman, which in this city was sometimes hard to find. But I believed that if I handled the situation like a lady, that I would be treated like one.

Nick called me, and we had dinner. He was feeling down, and it became more of a therapy session than a date. Nick needed a shoulder to lean on, and I really didn't mind being just that, as I felt no attraction towards him. I did feel sorry for him, and I admired him for caring so much about the welfare of his kids; he loved them dearly.

Nick drove me back to my house, kissed my cheek and thanked me for listening to him.

"How about you, Jenny, and I get together for dinner when I get back from Hawaii," he asked, "love to Nick, have a great time," I replied.

Nick sent me a Hula skirt and Jenny a lei from the islands. I called and thanked him when he returned, and we all got together for dinner.

"THE NAKED KISS"

Karen Conrad on the set

I was pushing my kids on the swings at the kiddie park in Beverly Hills, where we sometimes hung out.

"Push me higher, higher, mom," Chris cried out.

"Higher for me, too," Robin echoed him.

And on it went. I tried to take my kids somewhere every chance I got. I was still working part-time for Sam and going to the interviews for acting jobs my agent sent me on.

A man arrived with his two kids, who joined mine on the two empty swings next to us. Soon, the man and I found ourselves in a pushing race as the kids wanted to see who could go higher. The man and I ended up having a ball, laughing as much as the kids until we had to stop and catch our breath.

I was worn out, and the kids were hungry, so we made our way to one of the last empty park tables to have the snacks I had packed in our lunch bag.

The father and his kids came over and asked if he could share the table with us as there was no other available.

"Certainly, come join us," I said as I smiled and motioned them to sit on the bench across from us. After they had settled, I introduced myself and the kids.

The young father then introduced himself as Danny Simon and what he called his "two munchkins," Michael and Valerie.

The kids started talking to each other, and Danny and I started our adult conversation between the whoops and hollers from the kids who had finished their snacks, politely shared, and off they went to play in a sandbox nearby.

As Danny and I were getting to know each other, we finally started talking about what we each did for a living. I told him about my acting, modeling, and my part-time job a few nights a week at the ritzy Cave De Roy, a private club on La Cienega. That job would last only a few months until shooting began on Sam's movie, and the waitressing, with its late hours, left me worn out and took too much time away from my kids.

Danny told me he was a writer, recently divorced, who had just moved to Beverly Hills from New York. Danny was the brother of Neil Simon, who wrote the famed Broadway hit play, "Barefoot in the Park." I don't remember Danny and I ever dating except for play dates with the kids at the park, but we would talk on the phone every now and then and kept up a friendship.

Sam was ready to start shooting "The Naked Kiss" with Constance Towers, Anthony Eisley, and Michael Dante. I would have about two weeks on the set. We would still have dinner occasionally, and everything was back to the old relationship we had before Tim and Jim.

While filming the first movie, we all went to The Brown Derby restaurant on Vine Street and had the wonderful Cobb salad for which it was famous. We might start shooting at 6 a.m., and after dinner, we might get home by

8 p.m. Not the best schedule for a mother raising children. I would mostly have the weekends when the kids and I would drive out to see their grandparents in Glendora and spend a night or two.

There were a few other girls in Sam's movies that I knew he had had flings with. One was a beautiful actress from England named Marie Devereux, who was an Elizabeth Taylor lookalike. Marie had been in the movie "Cleopatra." She was the one who was rolled out in the rug instead of Liz, who apparently didn't do rug rollouts.

Marie had been cataloging books at Sam's when he and I first met. She wasn't around after I started working for him, but we would meet while filming Sam's movie "Shock Corridor." She was sweet and friendly and would also be in this movie.

Her character was named Buffy. My character was Dusty, very apropos, I would say.

Marie had a boyfriend, Larry, a photographer who was tall and handsome, who once made a pass at me saying, "Marie wouldn't mind." I remember my naive self thinking, "Oh, Larry, of course she'd mind!" as I knew I certainly would. (Later, I would learn just how open Marie turned out to be during a trip with Jenny Maxwell to Palm Springs.)

I was playing Dusty, a nurse in the movie who ends up getting pregnant. The main character, Kelly, played by Constance Towers, gave Dusty the money to leave town. I had a crying scene and another couple of speaking scenes. I was excited, but I worried I wouldn't be able to cry when the cameras rolled.

On the day of the crying scene, I was nervous as I waited to shoot the scene. I waited and waited, hours, it seemed. Finally, at the very end of the day, we were ready to shoot the scene where Dusty tells Kelly that she is pregnant, and I was to cry. Sammy knew what he was doing by keeping me on edge all day because I couldn't help but burst into tears at the right moment, and I cried and cried on the very first take.

I found out a week later that I really was pregnant when that scene was shot. I had an abortion as I could just barely take care of the two children I had. I was their only means of support.

***

One day during shooting, a few of the cast members and I went across the street from the studio to a well-known restaurant called Formosa, famous for its wonderful

Chinese food and ambiance. Our eyes had to get used to the dim light as we entered the Asian-styled restaurant, and the smells suddenly reminded us how hungry we were.

As we waited for our table, a man approached me, thinking I was someone else again. He smiled, then apologized and introduced himself as Sidney Miller, a well-known actor, director, and songwriter who had worked with Donald O'Connor in some of his song-and-dance movies. He was well-liked in the business and didn't have the reputation of being a womanizer.

Sidney apologized, and asked my name and whether I was an actress. I replied and then he asked whether I had a SAG card.

"I sure do," I said.

He asked about my agent, and I gave him a card with my agent's name and number.

"Well, I am sorry about the mistake," Sidney said. "It was nice meeting you, Karen Conrad." He smiled, turned, and walked out the door as we went to our table.

A co-worker asked if I knew who he was.

"Yes, that was Sidney Miller," I said and then uttered a big "wow," as it seemed like I was getting mistaken for a lot of other actresses, like Rita Moreno, when I had dark hair, and Angie Dickinson, Julie Christie, Donna Mills, and

Brigette Bardot when I was blonde. I joked that I was starting to wonder whether it was just a way for men to meet women.

My agent called the next day to say Sidney Miller wanted me to play a part in "My Three Sons" in an episode he was directing at the time. I thought about Tim and wondered if he was still on the show, as I had heard he might be leaving.

Unfortunately, I had to turn it down as it was shooting while I was working on Sam's movie.

(Isn't it interesting how being at the right place at the right time has everything to do with our lives? I seemed to be going that way in mine. I kept saying my mantra every morning: "I don't know what is on the way for me today, but I know it can only be good. I give thanks for all the good coming my way today.")

I was recommended by one of my friends for a day's shoot on a one-season series called "Channing." I was to play the girlfriend of the star, Jason Evers, on the last episode they shot. That paid for food and rent for the month.

On the set of "The Naked Kiss"

CLINT EASTWOOD – MARTONI'S

1st Row: Clint Eastwood, Kitty Jones & Richard Lee
2nd Row: Maggie Eastwood, James Brolin & Jane

My phone was ringing off the hook as I walked in the door. It was Kitty.

"Karen, are you busy Friday night," she asked. "I'm having a birthday dinner with Henry Jones, Clint, and Maggie. I want you there for the celebration."

"Kitty, you know I wouldn't miss your birthday dinner for anything in the world," I said. "You bet I'll be there."

The party would begin at 7 p.m. at Martoni's. Kitty told me Clint and Maggie were hosting.

"Don't worry about a thing," she said. "Just bring your sweet self."

"Kitty, you know I love you," I said. "I'll be there with bells on my toes. And thanks for the invite."

Kitty and I had become close, and she was the best friend a girl could want. There wasn't anything Kitty wouldn't do for a friend. She had the biggest heart of anyone I had ever met.

Kitty would marry Clint Eastwood's stuntman, Richard Lee, and would have two sons. They divorced in the '80s while living in Woodland Hills. Kitty had opened her own Employment Agency and, sadly, later, was diagnosed with kidney disease.

She later would be filmed in a T.V. show, as they were tracking her down when a kidney became available for her transplant. They just found her in time for the operation as she had been out of town. Kitty passed away a few years later and is missed by so many.

I liked Maggie Eastwood. We had become friends through Kitty, and in the years following her divorce from Clint, I would meet her and a few other friends for lunch with Kitty in Beverly Hills when she was in town.

Maggie was a major support to Clint through his climb to stardom. She was also the mother of his two children, Alison and Kyle. They were married from 1953 to 1984. I had all the respect in the world for her, and Clint knew that, during those early days as we socialized together, Clint was always a gentleman in my presence.

After her divorce from Clint, Maggie would later marry Henry Weinberg, an ex-boyfriend of Elizabeth Taylor. That marriage would only last a few years.

I loved Martoni's. I was friends with Tony Riccio, who was the co-owner, along with Mario Marino. The two had opened Martoni's in 1960. Their Italian restaurant would become a favorite of Frank Sinatra and the Rat Pack, along with Nat King Cole and the higher-ups in the music business.

I later found out that a family member of Tony's was a New York police officer who had looked after Sinatra's mother. Their relationship went back that far.

Martoni's was in a perfect location, between Sunset Boulevard and Hollywood Boulevard on Cahuenga Boulevard, an area where there were a lot of recording studios and record companies.

On the night of Kitty's birthday dinner, I walked into the restaurant and found Tony at the reservation stand at the entrance of the bar area. He gave me a warm hello and an even warmer hug. Tony was a hunk, tall, with wavy dark hair.

He led me into the large dining room with red leatherette booths you had to step up to get into. Clint Eastwood slid out along with his wife, Maggie, so I could slide in next to Kitty as Henry Jones was on her other side. I greeted Henry, Clint, and Maggie, and gave Kitty a hug and wished her a happy birthday.

Everyone in the room was watching our table, with Clint Eastwood sitting at the end with his long legs crossed and one foot hanging over the step.

Martoni's was decorated in the warm colors of Italy: red, green, and gold. Pictures of Italy in gilded gold frames hung on the walls. At the entrance was a mural of an Italian woman in the fields with a man next to her, which had been painted by a local artist, Tony Mafia. It always got attention as people entered the restaurant.

Kitty's party was a warm, friendly celebration with her closest friends. Clint and Maggie kept the conversation going with memories of previous celebrations. Henry was a long-time friend of Kitty's, a sweet, older actor who played character roles on TV. Clint told us to get whatever we wanted, and most of us ordered Tony's delicious pasta and wine.

We all sang "Happy Birthday" as Tony came in with the beautifully decorated birthday cake Maggie had ordered. Afterward, Kitty opened her cards and presents, exclaiming, "I love this, it's beautiful" and "just what I wanted" as the paper flew off her gifts. We knew she was enjoying every minute as she had such joy for life with whatever she did or wherever she was.

We all got up to say our goodnights and commented on the fun evening we all had shared. Kitty beamed as Clint gave her a hug and a kiss on the cheek as everyone in the room still had their eyes on him and our group.

Clint joined me a few times to keep me company and support Kitty when we'd be at some of the smaller clubs to hear Kitty sing, and we became friends.

Years later, in the late 70s, I was living in Indian Wells as I had re-married a man named Robert Rallo, a car dealer in the desert and living in the gated community of Indian Wells.

This was the year the Indian Wells Golf Club hosted the Bob Hope Golf Classic. I was there, watching the golfers from the sideline, and Clint was one of the golfers at the tee where I stood. After teeing off, Clint saw me, waved, and walked over to say hello.

We had a few minutes to catch up before he had to move on, and he asked whether I was going to be at the Club House dinner later that night. When I said I was, he suggested we meet up.

I went home to change to go back to the club for the dinner. As I walked in, Clint saw me and came over and gave me a hug. He led me to the table where David Soul and Mac Davis were chatting. We posed for pictures and stood there catching up for a few minutes.

Clint said he was glad to see me and invited me to a party at his place later.

"I'd love for you to come by," he said.

"I'd love to come," I told him, "But I think my husband has other plans for tonight. I'm sorry."

Clint looked disappointed. He gave me a goodbye hug, and we said goodnight.

I always knew Clint would be there if I called, but I never did.

Clint, Karen & David Soul

Karen & Clint

Clint & Kitty

FRANKIE VALLI, SONNY AND CHER, TONY RICCIO

Mario Marino, unknown, Tony Riccio & Karen Conrad

Tony Riccio and I had been friends for the past two years; it was nothing serious, as you could say he was married to his business. We all knew that owning a restaurant is a lot of work and very time-consuming, even with a partner.

Tony went out of his way to keep his customers happy, and Martoni's wonderful Italian food kept smiles on their faces. Sinatra and the Rat Pack were among those who would have food delivered to their homes at all hours for parties, as many Hollywood celebrities were Tony and Mario's loyal customers.

I don't think Tony had much time for socializing other than for a friend or customer who was involved in the opening of a movie or a social affair. Tony was not a drinker, as owning a business with a bar has been the downfall of many club and restaurant owners. Tony was too smart for that.

Occasionally, I would help Tony by answering phones on a busy night, and a little extra money would come my way.

One night, Tony called as I was fixing dinner for my kids. He said he and Mario had to make an appearance at The Coconut Grove the next night for Walter Winchell's birthday party.

"I was hoping you'd be free to go with us," Tony said. "Can you arrange for a sitter? I'll take care of it."

I told him it sounded like it would be a fun evening. I'd never been to the Grove. We made plans to meet at the restaurant at 5 p.m.

The Coconut Grove was a big, beautiful nightclub located in the Ambassador Hotel, full of the warm, old Hollywood ambiance, with the usual red and gold décor of the era, along with groves of green palm trees.

Tony and Mario led Mario's date and me to our table, from which we had a good view of the stage and the band behind where Walter Winchell would come up to the mike to thank everyone and give his greeting to all his friends, and he had many. The large room was packed with handsome men in tuxedos and beautiful, jeweled women in designer gowns with their hair done in the latest styles.

Tony and Mario would stand up and introduce Mario's date and me to their many friends and customers who came to our table to say hello. Everyone was friendly, and we had a wonderful time. Walter did his thing, and then a huge cake was brought up to him on the stage as the band played "Happy Birthday," and the crowd sang along. We all had a great time. It was another fun night with friends. I still have the photo that was taken that night. I was wearing the same black boatneck sleeveless dress that I'd worn to countless other events.

I met a lot of people through Tony. One regular, a record producer with a studio up the street, came in, and we started talking. I think his name was Ron, but it's been too many years to remember his last name. Anyway, I read him a poem I had written, and he said, "I really like this. Let me take it back to the studio and have my engineer see if he can put music to it." Ron came back about an hour later and asked me if I could sing. I really couldn't, but he got me into the studio, and I did a demo. I got a copy that I gave to my uncle as it had to be played on a big reel, which he had. I forgot all about it. Years later, I was sorry because I became a songwriter, and I'd let that earlier chance go by as I was dedicated to just being an actress.

One night, when I was helping Tony out, answering the phone, Tony got a call inviting him to see a young couple he was friends with at their first public performance. They would be the opening act a couple of nights later at Pandora's Box, a club down on Sunset Boulevard where it crossed with Crescent Heights.

Pandora's Box was a smaller, dark nightclub and coffeehouse in West Hollywood. It would be at the center of the Sunset Strip curfew riots in 1966 when it closed for good.

I met Tony at his restaurant, and we took his car and headed down Sunset to the opening of his friends, who were calling themselves "Caesar and Cleopatra." They were dressed in white and gold Grecian robes. Caesar had his gold laurel leaf crown, and Cleo had a gold band with a snake's head sitting on top of her long, raven hair with a fringe of bangs framing her beautiful face. Her black-lined eye makeup was perfect, as were her full red lips.

They were telling Tony how nervous they were, and Tony was trying to loosen them up and calm their jitters. After a trip to the lady's room, I walked up to Tony and his friends.

"Karen, I want you to meet my friends, Sonny and Cher Bono," Tony said.

"I'm so happy to meet you two," I said. "Tony has been telling me how talented you two are, and that you are on your way to a very successful career."

Tony wished them good luck, gave Cher a hug, and then shook Sonny's hand.

We left the two just in time to get to our seats before the music started.

"Tonight," a voice announced, "we have the pleasure of introducing the first-ever public performance of Caesar & Cleopatra. Give these two a hand, folks."

The spotlight followed the two as they came up to the mikes. They sang one song after another, loosening up with each other, and the crowd went wild.

This was the beginning of the road to fame for Sonny and Cher.

It was never boring at Martoni's. On another night, when I was working at the reservation stand, a young, good-looking Italian guy dressed in a suit asked if Tony was there. I motioned my head toward the kitchen.

"Tonys in there," I said. "One moment and I'll get him."

"No, it's okay," the man said. "He knows me. I'm an old friend."

He gave me a warm smile, turned, and made his way to the kitchen. A few minutes later, I heard laughter coming from the kitchen as the two then walked out and sat at the bar. Tony ordered a drink for his friend and a seltzer with lime for himself. I could tell by their friendly back-and-forth conversation that they had been friends for a while.

After his friend finished his drink, they came to where I was standing.

"Karen, I want you to meet my old buddy, Frankie Valli," Tony then said "Frankie, meet Karen Conrad."

"Karen, my pleasure, I was just asking Tony if he would let you leave work early," Frankie said. "I'm on my way to the Crescendo to catch a show as a favor to a friend, and I would love some company instead of just sitting there by myself, and Tony won't leave this place. How about it, Karen? Tony will vouch for me. You're in safe hands, right, Tony?"

"She had better be, Frankie, or else you know what will happen," Tony joked and then nodded his head with an OK in my direction.

"I'd love to go," I said. "Thanks."

I grabbed my purse and jacket; then Frankie led me outside and had the valet bring his car.

Traffic was heavy down Sunset to the Crescendo, but we got there on time and were led to our table, which gave us a good view of the stage. For the life of me, I can't remember who we saw; it may have been Don Rickles, as I had seen him before. Anyway, we had a light dinner and drinks, and I enjoyed his company, hearing stories about his early years before getting into the music business with his group, The Four Seasons.

After the show, Frankie took me promptly back to my car at Martoni's, saw me safely to my car, where he gave me a friendly hug and thanked me for going with him. "It's been a pleasure," he said. "Goodnight, Karen."

Martoni's

PALM SPRINGS – JENNY MAXWELL

My friend Jenny Maxwell decided we needed a getaway.

"How about it, Karen," she said. "Have you been to the Springs?"

She was referring to Palm Springs, and I told her that I hadn't and that I couldn't afford it.

"My son is going to be at his dad's this weekend, and didn't you say Robin and Chris are going with their grandparents to the ranch for two weeks?" she said.

I told her I was packing their clothes as we spoke.

"Well, I am ready for a getaway, and I think we both need a girls' trip. How about it, Karen?" "The sun, a nice massage, a night out, and an early to bed to catch up on some sleep. We both are due. Our kids will be away, so we might as well take advantage of it."

Jenny said the trip would be her treat.

"I'll reserve the room with two doubles, and I'll drive," she said. "In fact, I think we will be close to Glendora, and we could drop Robin and Chris off on the way out on the I-10 freeway."

"Oh, Jen, I can't let you do that," I said.

"Come on, Karen," she pleaded. "Let's do it."

"Okay, okay, you've twisted my arm," I said. "In fact, both arms, you wild woman."

Jenny laughed and told me she'd pick us up at 1 p.m., and to be ready.

I was through packing the kids' clothes and was starting in on what I was going to take when the phone rang,

It was Kitty.

"I just wanted to touch base with you about next weekend and the party I'm throwing on Saturday," she said.

"The kids will still be out of town, and I'll be there, I promise," I assured her.

"What are you doing this weekend?" she asked.

I told her Jenny, and I were heading to Palm Springs for a little getaway.

"The Springs, huh? I heard Tony's headed out to the Springs this weekend, too," Kitty said." You should give him a call. He usually stays at the Marquee, and I'm sure he'd love to take you and Jenny out to dinner."

"Good idea, Kitty," I said. "I just may do that."

I hung up the phone, thinking Tony was a trustworthy guy who was always fun to be around. We'd be in good hands for sure.

I was getting more excited about going away to the desert. This would be a first for me, and a change of scenery, some sun, and a massage sounded like pure heaven.

Jenny picked us up promptly at 1 p.m. We drove down Sunset to the on-ramp to the Hollywood freeway and through the civic center to the I-10. About 20 minutes later, we pulled off on Citrus Avenue in Covina and made our way toward the foothills, gray with smog. My mother always said it wasn't smog but smoke as San Gabriel Valley was the Indian valley of the smoke. I wasn't buying it.

I gave Rita a hug as she opened the door for the kids and me. They were so excited to drive back to the ranch, but they settled down enough to give me a goodbye hug and kiss.

"See you two in two weeks," I said. "I'll miss you guys. Have fun and be good for your grandparents. I love you."

It was always hard for me to have them gone that long, but it was wonderful they had the opportunity to travel, and I knew their grandparents would take good care of them.

Back in the white T-Bird with Jenny driving, we were off again and on the freeway to the Springs, stopping only once for gas. Driving for what seemed like hours, I watched the scenery change from buildings and green trees and foliage to wild, open space covered with what looked to me like blankets of sand, sagebrush, a tree or two, and cactus here and there, alone like soldiers standing guard near piled boulders where Indians may once have stopped to find shade from the hot summer sun.

I let my mind wander as I watched out the window. I saw run-down shacks here and there. We then crossed a large, dry riverbed. Soon, a few billboards advertising a hotel, or a casino appeared with the latest talent pictured on them, and finally, we came to the Palm Springs turn-off, which would take us down Palm Canyon Drive alongside the mountains on which the road ran parallel.

We made our way towards our turn, which was before the downtown area, where the next day, we would go to check out the small shops that lined both sides of the main street. Finally, we turned into the driveway of the Racquet Club, where we would be spending two nights, thanks to

Jenny. We parked the car, and while Jenny went in to register, I got our suitcases out and ready to be taken to our room.

It was a hot day. It was hotter than the city we had left, but it was a nice, soft, dry heat, and the pool looked inviting. Jenny and I went to our room, unpacked, and decided to lay out by the pool for a half hour or so, take a dip to cool off, and order drinks as we would have an early dinner at the club and make it an early night.

I remembered I was supposed to call Tony Riccio at the Marquee. As Jenny was using the bathroom to change into her two-piece white bathing suit, I picked up the phone and had the operator dial his hotel.

He answered on the second ring.

"Hey, handsome, it's Karen," I said.

"Karen, where are you? And how did you know I was here?" Tony asked.

"Kitty told me," I said. "Jenny and I drove down and are staying at the Racquet Club for the weekend."

"That's great," Tony replied. "I'm so glad you called me. Have you girls made any plans?"

I told him we were having a quiet night as we had just arrived, and then tomorrow it was sun, swim, and a downtown visit.

"Well, I'm taking you two ladies out to dinner tomorrow evening," Tony said. "I insist, Karen. Why don't you and Jenny meet me at the Metropole Restaurant tomorrow night, say 7?"

"That's so sweet of you!" I replied.

Tony replied: "My pleasure."

THE RAT PACK 1964 – "OH, WHAT A NIGHT!" – TONY RICCIO, FRANK SINATRA & DEAN MARTIN

By the next evening, we were sun-kissed, rested, and thoroughly shopped out! Jenny looked beautiful in her beige-and-white, lightly flowered summer dress with a white cardigan sweater. I was wearing my usual go-to dress, A-line, black, and sleeveless, but I was wearing something new! A wide-brimmed black hat I had found on sale at one of the high-end shops downtown. I felt very sleek and was looking forward to our night out.

Tony remarked how lucky he was to have two beauties on his arm as we followed the hostess to our table.

Promptly, the waiter came over and asked for our drink orders. Jenny and I each asked for a glass of white wine, and Tony ordered his usual non-alcoholic club soda with a twist of lime.

We chatted over our drinks and laughed as Tony told us the latest jokes. Tony appeared to be a different person when he was outside of Martoni's, or maybe the desert had worked its magic on this much more relaxed Tony.

The waiter suggested either steak or a special chicken dish. Tony and I both ordered the steak, while Jenny chose the chicken. The aroma of the food being served made us twice as hungry, as did watching the other tempting dishes pass by on their way to other diners.

The place was packed with well-dressed people laughing and 'oohing and ahing' over their beautifully plated meals. Chatter filled the large room, and a feeling of relaxation fell over Jenny and me. That's what the desert did for visitors from the busy city.

After our wonderful meal, Tony asked if we'd like an after-dinner cocktail. Jenny declined, saying she felt a headache coming, and she excused herself.

"Tony, would you mind bringing Karen back to the Racquet Club? I'd really like to go back now and get an aspirin for my headache, then turn in early," she asked.

"Of course not, Jenny," Tony said.

"Go, feel better, and I'll see you later," I said, feeling bad for my friend.

Tony stood up, walked Jenny to the front door, and gave the valet her ticket and a tip.

The waiter stopped Tony on his way back to our table, nodding his head in the direction of a large table at the back of the room and off to the side. I hadn't noticed the group before, so I turned around to check them out.

Tony nodded and smiled while looking toward the large group, and then he waved. Someone motioned him to come over. When Tony returned to our table, he asked if I wanted to join his friends, who had just invited us over for a drink.

"If you want to, Tony, it's okay with me."

I couldn't make out any faces from where we were, as the waiters were busy walking around, taking drink orders, and some of the guests were standing up and walking around, talking to the others at the table. Quite a party, I thought; Tony knew everyone.

Tony paid our check, and I picked up my purse and followed him across the room. Other people at tables nearby were looking over at this group, and I thought to myself someone important had to have been sitting there.

Tony took my hand and there we stood as he greeted the famed Rat Pack.

"Hey, Frank, Dean, Joey, Sam," Tony said. "Nice seeing you, Jilly. How's New York treating you? It's good seeing you again."

Sammy Cahn, a songwriter who had a string of hit recordings with Frank Sinatra and who won an Oscar for his song "Three Coins in the Fountain," greeted Tony.

"Everyone, meet my friend, Karen Conrad," Tony said.

Frank Sinatra motioned for us to sit down after the waiters made room, pulling up two more chairs. Tony sat across from me, and we were now on each side of Frank, who was seated at the head of the long table. I don't remember who was on the other side of Tony, probably Frank's girlfriend. Frank was hosting tonight's going away party for his girlfriend, who was leaving in the morning for Europe on a month-long vacation.

I looked over the brim of my hat into the smiling brown eyes of the person on the other side of me. It was the handsome, smiling Dean Martin.

"Hello, pretty lady," he said to me. "I love your hat, so I'm going to christen you 'The Hat' tonight as you really wear it well."

He was the sweetest, nicest man I would meet that night, softly spoken, and he put an extra beat in my heart with his warm and tender ways. I looked up at him with my blue eyes from under my hat, feeling a little flirtatious with this man.

He asked me questions about my life and if I was in "the business."

I told him about the films I'd been in, and we talked about his latest projects. I was in heaven, and I loved being 'The Hat' for the evening.

Tony was talking to everyone close to him, asking questions about what was up with Sammy Davis Jr. and Joey Bishop. He was familiar with everyone, and they all liked him.

Tony wasn't one to talk about his customers, but this group apparently loved his food. I heard comments about "missing your lasagna" and how wonderful his ravioli was. I knew he catered a lot of Beverly Hills parties, and what a good businessman that he was, Tony did well schmoozing with his customers.

They had already finished their dinners and were enjoying their drinks when Sammy Davis Jr. stood up and said, "Guys, it's time we take off for the airport."

Apparently, they were on their way to Vegas. Joey stood up and pushed his chair back.

Dean turned to me. "Unfortunately, Karen, I have to catch a plane, though I'd rather stay and talk to you," he said. "But I'm glad to have met you and keep wearing hats."

"It's been my pleasure," I said, "and thanks for my new title."

I told him I would remember to wear more hats and wished him a safe trip.

I longingly followed Dean with my eyes as the guys left.

***

Frank was still busy entertaining everyone, and I noticed there were probably fifteen or so people left at the table. Some moved in closer to Frank after the three left to catch their flight. Tony glanced at me across the table with a look asking if I was having a good time. I was listening to all the talk about Vegas shows, Frank's albums, Sammy Cahn's newest songs, and general show biz chatter. I gave Tony a thumbs up.

After the last round of drinks was finished, Frank, still ready to party, asked everyone if they'd like to join him at the Rim Rocks, which was on the way to his desert compound on Frank Sinatra Drive in Rancho Mirage.

Tony came over to me as I got up from the table and asked if I wanted to go with the group. I told him I'd be crazy not to. Tony and I chuckled, and off we went to follow Frank and his entourage. Since Tony didn't drink, I knew we would be safe driving. I was a sipper and had maybe a glass of wine an hour if that, so I was OK to party more with this fun group. I knew it was going to be a once-in-a-lifetime experience.

I was sorry Jenny had gone back to the hotel, and I hoped her headache was better. Maybe she had thought I wanted to be alone with Tony, but she knew we were not a couple and had never taken our friendship in that direction. She would certainly be sorry she missed the rest of this night.

We drove along Palm Canyon alongside the mountains; the moon was out and helped guide us to the road that led up to the parking area behind the famed Rim Rocks Restaurant and Nightclub, where we'd found Frank and his friends at the bar ordering drinks.

"Tony, Karen, what are you two drinking," Frank asked. "Yeah, I know, Tony, only seltzer for you, with lime. Karen, how about a Black Russian? According to the ladies I know, I hear it's a popular after-dinner drink." Frank chuckled as we joined the group, which was now down to about twelve people, and we listened to the jazz group playing.

Frank held court, keeping everyone on their toes with stories, going back and forth among the group until about an hour later, some of the group called it an evening and made their way home. Frank invited Tony and me, along with a few other night owls, to continue the party at his house, which wasn't far from Rim Rocks. Apparently, Frank liked to party, and we were on for the ride.

FRANK SINATRA'S HOUSE – YUL BRYNNER

It was close to 12:30 when Tony and I got to Sinatra's modern, flat-roofed house that stood back from the street, barely lit, in the desert night. We walked to the front door, rang the bell, and were greeted by a man who worked for Frank in some capacity.

We could hear the people at the end of the entranceway, which opened to a large, long room in the back. The kitchen was on the right side of the front of the house, and apparently, the bedrooms were to the left. We were led back and found the large room that had a fireplace and seemed to be where everyone was mingling. Across from the fireplace wall was a half-opened, draped wall with glass sliding doors that led out to the lighted swimming pool. Further back, I could see a slightly lit, roundish, small building to the right. I could barely make out another one on the left as it was dark.

After we entered the room, Tony went to get me a drink, taking my coat down a hallway to a room off to the side of the kitchen, which I presumed was an additional bedroom, maybe the staff's quarters.

I looked around and noticed a few of the people from the group had apparently gone home. It was getting late, but about eight or so had hung in. I heard a female voice ask, "Karen, is that you?"

I turned to see Marie Devereux, standing there in a loose caftan, looking as beautiful as ever, though she was make-up-free, and her hair looked a bit rumpled. We hugged and said hello, taking a few minutes to catch up. Apparently, she was a guest, maybe a friend of Frank's girlfriend, though she had stayed back at the house instead of joining the party for dinner. I didn't ask and felt it was her business.

A few more people who weren't at the dinner joined the group. Tony came back with our drinks and Yul Brynner, the star of the movie "The King and I," to whom I was introduced.

Wow, I thought, this is really a treat. I had met more major stars tonight than in my whole time in Hollywood. What a night to remember.

Frank then called to me: "Karen, come over and sit next to me, tell me about yourself. We really haven't had much of a chance to talk."

He patted the empty chair next to him as he sat closest to the fireplace. A large coffee table sat in front of our chairs, with other chairs placed around it in a wide U-type setting.

I looked over at Tony, but he was busy talking to people I didn't know, so I walked over to Frank, put my drink and my small purse on the coffee table, and sat down in the chair next to my host.

"Where is the guest of honor," I asked Frank. "I was hoping to wish her Bon voyage before I left the club, but I didn't get the chance."

"She's off packing and getting ready," Frank said. "She has an early flight and still has to drive back to LA."

"Well, I'm sure she enjoyed her sendoff party," I said. "It's been a lovely evening, and I want to thank you for inviting Tony and me to be part of it."

Frank swirled his chair around toward me, reached over, and patted my arm, which rested on the rim of my chair next to his; I swirled my chair around to face him as we talked. We chatted for about 20 minutes about the kidnapping of his son, Frank Jr., and what they went through to get him back. It had been a nightmare that no parent should ever have to live through.

I was smoking at that time and reached over to get a cigarette out of my purse. Frank reached over to pick up a lighter on the table and lit my cigarette.

"I like you, Karen, and would like to get to know you," he said.

"Isn't that what we're doing?" I replied as I smiled and nervously took a puff off my cigarette, wondering what I'd gotten myself into.

I changed the subject to his latest album and figured he would be happy to talk about his music instead of me, which he was until I stood up to reach over to the ashtray to put my cigarette out.

Frank reached for my hips and pulled me down.

"Karen, sit here on my lap," he said.

I told him I didn't think that would be a good idea as I politely removed his hands and took my body back to my own seat.

"Frank, I don't want to be an embarrassment to Tony, who is a friend of yours," I said. Frank kind of nodded but didn't seem pleased about not getting his way, something I am sure he wasn't used to. "And, Frank, this is a party for your girlfriend, and these are some of her friends, and I wouldn't want to hurt her feelings."

He took in my words and slowly nodded again.

He then said, "Karen, it's a hot summer night, and if you like, why don't you take a swim in the pool?"

I told him I didn't have a bathing suit, and he said he keeps some around for his guests. With that, he walked to his bedroom and came out with a new bathing suit that would fit me, as well as a terry robe and a towel.

I looked around for Tony, but he was still nowhere to be found. I felt abandoned and ill at ease with Frank's advances, and I needed to get out of there.

Frank directed me through his bedroom to his bathroom, where I changed into the suit, which fit. I guess he measured my hips for it when he pulled me down to his lap. I giggled as that thought crossed my mind.

One thing that didn't cross my mind at that time was that he could have had a two-way mirror, or that he was filming me nude. I wanted out of this situation one way or another.

So, I took the robe and towel and went out the sliding door and swam in the cool, clear water, looking up at the night sky, and took myself to another place; I chilled out under the stars outside instead of inside with the stars under a roof.

After about 30 minutes, I got out of the pool and dried off. Sliding the glass door open, I walked back in and found a few stragglers left in the room. Frank was saying goodnight to his guests as he was turning in. He hugged me and whispered in my ear that he wanted my phone number.

"Please leave it for me," he said.

I thanked him for a wonderful evening and went looking for Tony. I also had to get my clothes, which I had left in Frank's room. I was tired, and it was late. I wanted Tony to take me back to the hotel.

Tony was nowhere to be found. Nobody had seen him. I went into the kitchen and found Marie. I told her I had been looking all over for Tony and that nobody knew where he was.

"His car is still here, and he's not," I told her. "I don't know what to do or even where I am. I could call Jenny to come get me, but I can't leave without Tony."

"Karen, don't worry," Marie said. "Someone told me Tony passed out, and the guys put him in the guest room off the kitchen. It's going to be okay; he just needs to sleep it off."

"Tony passed out! I don't believe it, Marie," I said. "How could he? Tony doesn't drink, so how could he pass out?"

My head was spinning with all this as I knew Tony, and he wouldn't drink and leave me stranded. That wasn't the Tony I had known for the past two years.

"Come on, Karen, you can sleep in my bed tonight. Tony can take you back when he wakes up in the morning," Marie reassured me in her English accent.

I was tired and upset at this whole situation. Marie went to grab my purse and cigarettes off the coffee table. She then led me back through the sliding glass doors to the round building where I had seen the light through the window.

I saw the bed and couldn't wait to sleep.

"Goodnight. I'll see you in the morning," Marie said. "Don't worry, Karen."

And off she went into the starlit night to sleep, where I did not know or care.

Off came the white terry robe and the still-wet swimsuit, and off came the make-up with the washcloth I found in the bathroom, and under the cool, white sheets, I slid, breathing a sigh of relief as I quickly drifted into dreamland.

I was in the middle of a dream, lying on a warm sandy beach with a lover who was gently rubbing his fingers up and down my arm while his body cuddled like a spoon next to mine. I moaned a little as his fingers slipped closer and closer to my bare breast and started making circles around my hardening nipple. I felt his hot breath on my neck, which added to the stirring of passion.

I suddenly woke in the dark room and then, startled, reached over to turn on the light, but I knocked the lamp over with a loud crash before I could.

I wasn't alone in the bed.

Had Tony awakened and come in? Surely Tony wouldn't climb into my bed, would he? I slowly turned over and raised my hand to feel the person's face, and I moved my hand up farther, finding a bald head.

Yul... Yul Brynner was in my bed! Now, he was trying to calm me down after he turned on the other bedside lamp, and I could see his face.

"Yul, what are you doing in my bed?"

"Karen, I am attracted to you, and I want to make love to you. You're a beautiful, warm woman, born to be made love to," he said in an inviting, sexy voice. "We Europeans are hot-blooded and well-versed in pleasing a woman. Karen, you just might like it."

"Yul, I just might be tempted, and yes, I'm very flattered. But this American woman kind of likes the guy she came here with and is worried about what happened to him," I said. "I wouldn't want to embarrass or hurt Tony in any way, so tempted or not. I can't let you make love to me."

"Chéri, I will respect your wishes," he said. "Tony is a lucky man to have a beautiful friend such as you."

He kissed my hand, got up, and handed me the robe at the end of the bed.

"Karen, why don't you join me by the pool and watch a beautiful sunrise," he said as I slipped into the robe to cover my naked body.

We did just that, and it was beautiful. The morning sun came over the purple San Jacinto mountains, warming up the chilly morning air.

Yul and I chatted like old friends about the death of Marilyn Monroe, how heartbroken he and Frank were, and how much Frank had cared about her. We talked about Frank's relationship that ended with Peter Lawford, due to a change of plans regarding JFK's visit to Frank's compound. Things had been changed from Frank's house to Bing Crosby's, and Frank was not happy with Peter or, apparently, Robert Kennedy. We even talked a bit about the mob and Frank's friend Sam Giancana.

The sun was up, and after a few hours or so of lounging and chatting on chaise lounge chairs, Yul offered to cook me breakfast. So, we went inside to Frank's kitchen, both of us in white terry robes, and Yul, who apparently enjoyed cooking, made us a wonderful, English-style breakfast with eggs, bangers, fried tomatoes, and sautéed mushrooms. A quite, yummy meal served with a large mug of coffee.

I asked Yul where my clothes were. He found them and brought them to me so I could dress back at the guest house.

"Thank you, Yul, you're a wonderful cook and a gentleman," I said.

Yul smiled and kissed me on the cheek.

"I wish it could have been different, chéri," he said. "You would have enjoyed me making love to you."

"I'm sure I would have, Yul" I said as I smiled and blew him a goodbye kiss as I went to dress before searching for Tony.

I was dressed and back in the kitchen having a refill on my coffee before looking for Tony when he came walking in, looking completely spaced out.

"Karen, are you okay? I am so sorry," he said. "I don't know what happened. I was talking to Yul in the kitchen while he freshened his drink and poured me a fresh soda. We talked for a little longer, and I remember telling him I needed to go check on you. I was on my way to find you, and I don't know what happened after that. The next thing I knew, I woke up this morning in a strange bed. What in the hell happened, Karen? What did you do when you couldn't find me?"

I told him all about my evening on the ride back to the hotel. The poor guy kept saying how sorry he was for putting me in that position and flaking out on me.

Jenny couldn't believe our stories, and we laughed and talked about the 'what ifs' that could have happened if I had said yes instead of no.

A few years down the line, after Tony and I had lost touch, I moved to Indian Wells, where I heard Tony had opened another restaurant in addition to the one he had opened at the Marquee in Palm Springs. I went to Riccio's, which was his new restaurant, located on Palm Canyon Drive on the way into Palm Springs.

Tony was happy to see me, and we had a great catch-up session, including the solution to the mystery of Tony passing out that night. Tony had been told (I believe by Sinatra) that if Yul saw a woman that he wanted to have sex with, and if he could get away with slipping knock-out drops to the guy she was with, he would do it.

Tony was upset remembering Yul in the kitchen refilling his soda that night, but he was glad that he finally had the answer as to why he passed out, as he hadn't had a drink.

He thanked me for saying no to Yul. We laughed as we looked back at that crazy night in the Springs.

***

Years later, as a songwriter, I would be introduced to Frank Sinatra Jr. when he was appearing at a club in Studio City. We chatted during his break, and he asked for my phone number, which I gave him as I was now divorced. He called and asked me to dinner. I said I'd meet him at the restaurant, and he gave me the name of a coffee shop on Lankershim Boulevard in Van Nuys. We met for dinner, and I found him very different from his father. He was very shy and not easy to be with; it was like having to draw the real person out of this solemn man.

It was interesting that this coffee shop was where he would go every night for dinner. It was a strange encounter and one I did not care to repeat. He would call and leave me messages asking me to join him again at the same coffee shop for dinner. I finally returned his calls and had to listen to some strange, eerie music on his message machine. I left a message saying I had started dating someone new. He was probably a nice guy, but I had learned to watch out for those red flags. He looked so much like his father and had talent, but sadly, he was cursed with his father's legacy, one that he could never live up to.

ELVIS PRESLEY – BEL AIR, PELUGIA WAY – APRIL/MAY 1964

The movie "Elvis" had been out for a while at the time of my writing this chapter. My friends asked if I saw it, and, if so, what did I think?

I hadn't watched it. I finally gave in, streaming it on HBO, watching from my cozy, warm bed on a cold Friday night.

What did I think?

Austin Butler reminded me more of Ricky Nelson as far as looks, and he did one hell of a job dancing in Elvis's boots, but there was only one Elvis. Only one pair of lips could curl up in his impish, got-you smile and kiss you as if it were his first kiss, tenderly touching your cheek with his fingers. Only one set of lashes could flutter over his sexy eyes, which looked through to your soul. Only one Elvis now and forever, in my opinion.

At the end of the movie, when the real Elvis sang "Unchained Melody" in a clip from his last Vegas show, it really hit me, and I cried for a man with whom I once shared a thread of my life for more than a moment in time.

I always knew this would be the hardest chapter to write. You always wonder if it is fate or chance that brings another person and chapter into your life. This one was Elvis Presley, and the year was 1964, and the place was Bel-Air, California. Elvis was in town working on the movie "Roustabout" with Barbara Stanwyck. A movie, he hoped, would give him more of a serious stance due to the stature of his co-star.

Kitty and I had been friends for a while by this time, and one evening, she called.

"I've got a surprise for you," she said. "Get yourself pretty, and I'll pick you up about 7."

I asked if she could give me a little hint about what was to happen.

She told me just to get ready. "You won't be disappointed."

Right at 7, Kitty honked her horn outside my house, and off I went to join her and her big surprise. That was Kitty, full of fun and spur-of-the-moment surprises that made her such a fun, loving friend who would be a part of my life until her death at an early age, a few years after getting a kidney transplant.

We chatted about what our days had been like as we drove from my little home in Hollywood, past the Sunset Strip, to Beverly Hills, and from there to Bel Air and up the street to a gated driveway that led to a beautiful, modern house on Perugia Way, where Elvis lived during his Los Angles stays.

"Come on, girl, you're going meet Elvis," she announced as we came to a stop at the end of the long driveway.

"Oh, my God, Kitty, "I exclaimed. "You've got to be kidding."

"Nope," she replied. "But you can't say anything about having two babies, and you can't sleep with him and become just another lay."

"Ok, ok, I'll just meet him, which will be just fine," I said.

I promised I wouldn't do either.

"You know how I don't want to be called easy in this town where I fight that image every day," I said. "And I'm sure he has far prettier women than me in his sights who would sleep with him at the drop of a compliment.

"Besides, Kitty, we mothers can't hide a few stretch marks," I joked."

Don't be silly," she replied with a twinkle in her eye. "He will love you. I know Elvis."

I had never been a major Elvis fan. I loved his ballads but had never bought a record. I had also never seen an Elvis Presley movie until my friend Jenny Maxwell, her mother, and I went to a drive-in to see her co-star with Elvis as the spoiled blond in "Blue Hawaii." That was the one and only Elvis movie I had seen.

My grandmother, Sweetie, would play his albums, and she loved his vocals. That had been my only exposure to

Elvis I had at the time, besides hearing him on the radio. Never in my wildest dreams did I ever think I'd meet him, let alone spend hours making out with him alone in his bedroom one day!

We were met at the door by one of the 'Memphis Mafia,' Elvis's bodyguards, stand-ins, and buddies. I don't remember which ones I met first, maybe Red or Sonny West (who were cousins), or Joe Esposito, Ray, or one of the others, as there were always more than a few around as I was to find out.

I felt like a scared rabbit as we walked into a large room. The first thing that caught my attention was a round fire pit. Over it hung a cone-shaped metal dome that was attached to the ceiling. My eyes then traveled farther to a large den area, where people were sitting on a huge, long, curved, red couch that seemed to cover the entire wall of the room.

The group on the couch sat spellbound as they watched Elvis standing in front of the TV set across the room, entertaining everyone with some big story he was acting out. The lights were dim with a red glow, and there was a jukebox and a big mahogany pool table, and there was Elvis.

He stopped, grinned, walked over to us across the thick, white carpet, kissed Kitty on the cheek, and then turned to me with a big, sexy smile.

"Hello there, pretty girl," he said.

I was twenty-two, and he was almost twenty-nine. I had never seen a man as beautiful as Elvis. He had the sexiest lips I would ever see, and his twinkling, flirty eyes lit up as they found mine.

"So, you're Karen," Elvis said. "Our friend Kitty has been telling me about her beautiful friend that I should meet. Come on in and join the others."

With my knees shaking, I entered 'Elvis Land' and a romance with Elvis Presley that would never be forgotten.

***

The guys were very protective of Elvis that first night. I saw him as the star he was, cracking jokes and overseeing the action. I began to feel more at ease as Elvis smiled and winked at me now and then, and the guys and their girls all made me feel at home, a part of the group. There were even some of the crew and cast members from the movie "Roustabout" that Elvis was filming at the time, who seemed to be at home with the group.

Kitty had to work the next morning, and after a few hours, she motioned that we needed to leave. Elvis walked us to her '55 Chevy, parked next to his big Caddies, and after taking my hand, he leaned down to kiss my cheek.

"I want to see you again," Elvis said. "Can I get your phone number from Kitty?"

I looked into those eyes of his and knew I was in deep trouble.

Driving back to my house, I told Kitty that Elvis could charm the pants off any woman.

"I think I might be in over my head," I told her. "Do you really think he'll call me? God, Kitty, what have you gotten me into? I didn't think this all would happen, that he'd ask for my number and want to see me again. You and your surprises, Kitty, nothing could be better than meeting that gorgeous man."

Kitty gave me a smile.

"He'll call you," she said. "Girl, he was taken by you, but you must remember, don't let him get into your panties or that will be the end of it. That's just the way he is. And no telling anyone you're seeing him. If the press finds out, it's over. And don't mention your kids."

"Okay, Okay, but why the secrecy about the kids," I asked.

"Karen, just do as I say and enjoy the time that you'll spend with him," she said. "Listen to Momma Kitty."

"Got it" I replied, still feeling a warm glow from his touch, and doing that magical thinking, that maybe I'll be different; after all, life is filled with memories, and these memories with him would always be mine to cherish.

***

Two nights later, Elvis called and asked me if he could see me the next night. I couldn't help but say yes.

"Honey, why don't you wear that blue sweater you wore last time," he said. "I really liked that with your blue eyes."

What a memory he had.

Elvis said Jimmy Kingsley would pick me up at 8 p.m.

"I'm looking forward to seeing you, baby," he said, and then he put Jimmy on the phone so I could give him directions to my house.

I must have sat there for an hour, taking it all in, feeling excited, scared, and unsure. I asked myself if I was enough to be in this man's obit, along with all the other beautiful, talented women he had been dating.

"Oh, my God! What will he think when he hears about this rundown house where I rent the back three rooms from the elderly owner who lives in front," I asked myself. "And what will I wear?"

I didn't have much in my small coat closet.

Why me?

It was then that I reminded myself about the book and the mantra that I repeated every morning: "I don't know what is on the way for me today, but it can only be for my good. I give thanks for all the positive goodness that will come my way."

"Think those positive thoughts, Karen," I said to myself. "He called and that means something. Enjoy the moments for what they are, for that is all we have in this life. This happened for a reason, and this is but another lesson in your path. It somehow seems I either learn or teach with each encounter."

Two nights later, with the kids at the sitter's, I looked through my meager wardrobe. The best I had was a black skirt and a matching black cape to wear with the blue sweater I had worn before. I had the cape and skirt made with some of the money from my first movie role. My friend Jenny had a beautiful one in a camel color; I had mine made by the same seamstress. It was very stylish for the time, and now I found myself thinking, "black with a cape." It was like I was sourcing Elvis with my cape.

Jimmy knocked on my front door and we chatted briefly as he led me to the big Cadillac and opened my door so I could slide into the black leather seat. This was the start of my dates that would continue for the next couple of months., from McCadden Place to the Bel Air gated driveway and into the arms of Elvis Presley.

Elvis usually would be in the den with the gang, looking like a Greek god, full of energy and laughter. He always was the center of attention, entertaining everyone with his wit and charm. When a girl was with Elvis, he was what you looked at, not the details of your surroundings.

Sometimes, he would pull out a pistol and twirl it around his finger and play cowboy, pointing it here and there as if he were going to shoot someone as he stood in front of the TV and his audience sat on the long, red couch.

Sometimes, he might show a little anger at one of the boys and stomp off into another room, but usually, he was happy being at home with his guys, yet I could tell he had a restlessness that would be hard to tame.

He had a thing about guns, and I later heard that one of Kitty's friends had been at his house when he was playing around with a .22. He put it to her head and scared the daylights out of her. She said he then turned and pointed the gun at the TV, pulled the trigger, and shot it to pieces.

Sometimes we'd sit and watch a show with the others, as the boys would always have the TV on, watching "Perry Mason," "Combat," or some other Elvis favorite. Then, after a while, he would reach out and grab my hand.

"Let's you and I get out of here," he'd say. "I want to be alone with you.

He would lead me into his bedroom, where the dimmed lights glowed a soft red, and to the big bed that was covered by a dark red, velveteen bedspread. This was where we would talk about movies, life, and dreams. His first kiss was gentle and sweet, and we played at being teenagers on a first date until he turned the passion into touching and feeling.

Elvis had a lot of questions when I told him about the mantra I would say every morning. He always seemed to want to learn. We talked about being positive and ways of looking at life, but we always would put the conversation aside and play kissy face until we would fall on our backs and get our breath back.

There were sliding glass doors in his room that led to the pool area outside. When it wasn't too cold, we would slip outside and sit on the grass and when we weren't making out, we might watch for a falling star or two.

Elvis had a thing about feet, and he told me that his mother loved for him to rub hers.

"Come on, girl," he'd say. "Let me see those feet of yours."

So, I'd remove my shoes and nylons, and I would let him rub my feet, cuddle, kiss them, and sometimes suck on my toes. Elvis seemed to think my feet were special and pretty. He called them 'Woddie Sooties,' a name he first called his mother's feet as a young boy.

We would let the passion get to a point where I would have to stop him over and over until we both laid back and came back down to earth. I had promised Kitty about not going 'all the way' with him, and I kept my word, as difficult as it was. My stockings and shoes would be the only items of clothing to leave my body during my time with Elvis.

Elvis never pushed it and respected my feelings about not going all the way. He would raise my sweater up or undo a few buttons of a blouse until my hand would stop him. Sometimes, I would let him feel my breast and kiss the part that peeked over the top of my white bra. It's just a thought, but from my experience with him, maybe he loved the foreplay just as much as the real thing.

It could be hot and wild. It could be sweet and silly. It could be painful with desire; it could be all a girl ever dreamed a lover could be. It was all this and more.

I was truly swept away with every kiss from those sweet lips along with the shivers from each tender, searching touch. He was everything, and it was killing me as I knew it could never go further for so many reasons. He was a star who would always have women throwing themselves at him and he was only human, and I was a woman with kids....

It was heartbreaking, knowing these moments couldn't last; it was heartbreaking that it had gotten this far.

Jimmy was the only one of the boys who would pick me up and take me home, and we always talked about how our days had been, but I always felt I could never overstep with any questions about Elvis. One day, I got the nerve to ask him if Elvis would ever marry Priscilla, as I had heard the on-and-off-again rumors.

Jimmy said Elvis wasn't ready to get married and that she was underage when her parents allowed her to move in. He left it up in the air, and I didn't pursue the subject any further.

***

One night, I wore a dress with a black slip underneath. When I sat down on the couch with the others, the lace from my black slip was showing, and this caught Elvis's eye, and not in a good way.

"Don't you ever wear black again," he said. "Don't you know, only bad women wear black?"

I had to think he meant lingerie and my slip, as all the women in his life wore black. What was this about? I was shocked and embarrassed. I felt like I wanted to hide after this strange outburst, as I had never heard anything like this before, but I kept quiet. I wasn't raised in the South with the strict religious background, rules, and ties to a mother as Elvis had been.

I suddenly saw the side of this man who worshiped his mother and her teachings. This was a part of Elvis I hadn't seen before, and there would be another that has always stood out to me.

After another sweet night together, Elvis was walking me out to the car. Somehow, we got to talking about cars. Whatever brought that subject up, I'll never know, but when I mentioned that I liked little cars, he flew off the handle, and just like that, he stormed away. I was left standing there, not understanding what had happened. Apparently, another side of Elvis was his quick temper.

Jimmy came to my rescue as I stood there alone and stunned.

"Come on, it's OK," he said. "I've got the keys. I'll take you home. Elvis lets his temper run away with him at times. Don't feel bad. Sometimes, just the smallest thing can set him off. I've been there, Karen; it's just something in him. It's not you. He really likes you, don't worry."

Jimmy walked me to my door that night and gave me a reassuring hug as we said goodnight.

I was sure that was to be the last time I would see Elvis. I did not know at the time that he had gotten involved with uppers and downers when he was in the Army, and this might explain his endless energy, moodiness, and quick temper.

Elvis ended up calling me the next night and apologizing for his outburst. He said he hoped I would see him again. And, yes, I accepted his apology, and, yes, I'd see him again.

On the next date, he came to pick me up in his big, black Rolls Royce, driven by Jimmy, who came to the door to get me. He opened the door to the car, and there sat a grinning Elvis with a gun in his lap.

Oh no, did my McCadden Place home worry him? I must have turned red.

"Elvis, what are you doing with a gun in your lap," I asked.

"Honey, I always carry a gun," he said. "You don't know how many people would come up to my window and try to break it in so that they could say that they hit Elvis Presley."

"Oh, no, people really do that?" I asked.

"Yeah, baby, they sure do. I never go out without my gun, and that's another reason the boys are always with me: I don't like to go out in public."

My heart broke for this man who had everything but lived in fear because he was born with a talent he chose to share with the world. He lived a life that no one could really relate to. He handled the love for his fans the best he could until the pressure of it all took him down.

That night, sitting in his car, he looked at the old white wooden frame house I shared, put his arm around me, and pulled me in close.

"Honey, don't you ever be ashamed of where you live," he said. "Never again, promise me, baby."

I promised him that I wouldn't.

I hadn't wanted him to see where I lived, but that night, in his Rolls Royce, his sweet words touched my heart, and my embarrassment slipped away.

Elvis was a man who would sometimes let his innocent boy side come through, the boy who loved his mother until the day he died, crushed by the greed of man. He was one of God's angels, sent to earth to bring the beauty of music and his spirit to this world in the short time he had on this planet. It's a gift we haven't seen since his passing.

Elvis had his moments when he would show his impish side, like when he would stand up and say "Ladies and germ-a-men" instead of gentlemen. He could pronounce it perfectly, so you would think it was gentlemen. It was one little bit of his silly side that I was to witness.

***

I had to add this to my Elvis chapter as I have just re-read the book I was in, called "Down at the End of Lonely Street," written by Peter Harry Brown and Pat H. Broeske. It tells of the guys having access to a bathroom mirror on the opposite side of his bedroom wall. That wall was across from the end of his bed.

I remembered this as I read about this mirror because I always wondered why there were two doors from which you could access his bedroom off the den: one was in his bedroom, and the other was located off the hallway leading to the bedroom. Now I might have the answer to my question and thank God I kept my clothes on.

***

I knew it was only a matter of days before Elvis would finish his scenes in "Roustabout" and leave Hollywood to head back to Graceland. We never spoke of his leaving, but I knew it would happen soon. That and my 'secret' weighed heavy on my heart.

There hasn't been anyone since Elvis who could take my breath away with his kisses and make me feel as if he was singing only to me with his beautiful voice while having those sexy eyes reach deep into my soul. Elvis was one of a kind. I will always be grateful for every moment I was given to spend with him.

I knew the end had to come. And it did. One night, Kitty called to tell me that Elvis found out about my kids. Someone sent him a letter. Kitty said he went ballistic. He told her she should have known better. And he told her that he had really liked me.

It hurt more than I thought it would, but I knew the day was coming. Things were getting to a point at which I knew I couldn't go on keeping a part of my life from him; after all, how much longer could I keep saying "no" to this man? It was the hardest thing I ever had to do.

I always wondered if Jenny Maxwell wrote the letter. She had been the only person I had told. I later heard she had had a crush on Elvis, but because she had a son, he wouldn't date her.

After, the press found out and I finally agreed to do an interview for Motion Picture magazine. I hated the headline, the photo, and the story. It turned out not to be what it should have been, in my opinion. I was sorry I had agreed to talk to the man who wrote it. I also was mentioned in the book I spoke of earlier.

Years later, Kitty Lee Jones, June Graham, Joni Lyman (who also knew Elvis), and I did a T.V. interview for "Entertainment Tonight." Only Kitty and I were in the final cut that was shown on TV.

Jimmy and I had become good friends with my pick-ups and drop-offs. I never saw him after it ended with Elvis. He was a stuntman and stand-in for Elvis, as well as a very nice guy that I felt completely at home with. I always wondered what happened to him.

Years later, I would find out. I was with June Graham, a friend of Kitty's. June had also met Elvis a few years later. While in Las Vegas, we ran into Red West at a casino, and when I asked what had happened to Jimmy, he told me a heartbreaking story.

Jimmy had committed suicide. He had an accident while filming a car chase that left him paralyzed. It happened shortly after he had gotten married, and his new wife left him for a drummer.

My heart broke in two for the nice, down-to-earth man with whom I had shared confidential moments on my trips home from visiting Elvis.

I'd like to think that today, Elvis would say: "Karen, you cared about your kids, and that was what was important. Good for you, baby."

Elvis Girls

Taken at the recording of "Entertainment Tonight"

Joni Lyman, June Graham, Karen Conrad, Kitty Jones Lee

HOLLYWOOD - GOODBYE?

Two months later, I left Hollywood to spend more time as a mother. I was asked by my girlfriend in Orange County to go to Hollywood one night to the Whiskey A Go Go. It had recently opened, and I hadn't been there yet.

From the street, we could hear the loud music and the wild crowd. As we started to walk in, I was stopped at the door by Danny Simon, my old friend from the kiddie park.

We stepped back outside where we could talk.

"Karen, I've written a script that's being made into a TV series," Danny said. "There's a part I think you'd be perfect for. The director is Lester Colodny, who is in the hospital after having surgery. All you must do is go meet him at the hospital, and the job is yours."

I was shocked and surprised.

Here was the chance I had waited years for. I hugged Danny, thanked him, and I said I'd go see Les.

I was quiet on the way home, thinking about this opportunity as I had heard Danny was working all the time on all the comedy shows, including, of all things, "My Three Sons."

The day I was to go into Beverly Hills to the hospital to meet Les, I drove onto the freeway. A few miles in I thought about my kids and the long hours I would have to be on the set when I was working.

It wasn't the life I wanted for them. I was all they had. And I realized I wanted the family I didn't have as a child. Maybe it would be just the three of us, but I wanted to be there for them.

I exited at the next off ramp, and I went back to my apartment to call Danny and tell him I wasn't interested in going back to the business.

BEVERLY HILLS - JENNY MAXWELL'S MURDER 1981 – TIP ROEDER, LEONARD MAIZLISH, GENE RODDENBERRY, PAUL RAPP

It's funny how threads of relationships past can suddenly appear and dangle in your face again years later. That would be the case with Jenny Maxwell and me.

In the '80s, I was dating an attorney named Leonard, who was friends with and represented Gene Roddenberry of "Star Trek" fame. Leonard's other best friend and client was Paul Rapp, Jenny Maxwell's first husband. Paul would be co-producing with Roddenberry on the filming of "Genesis II" due to my friend Leonard.

A few years earlier, Nick Adams had committed suicide. He had been the best friend and client of Jenny Maxwell's second husband, Tip Roeder, who discovered Nick's body after seeing him lying on the floor of his house through a window.

Nick's ex-wife, Carol, ended up married to Paul Rapp, Jenny's first husband. That marriage lasted just two years. Paul ended up raising Brian, Jenny's son.

Jenny and Tip's marriage was a dark and rocky one, as I would find out after talking on the phone with Jenny a few times when we re-connected. Jenny invited me to their home on a street off Mulholland Drive.

"Karen, this man threw me out of our house in the middle of the night," Jenny said. "I was lucky enough to grab my fur coat or I would have been standing outside completely naked. I need to get out of this, but Tip will never let me have anything, and how can I support myself at this age?"

Jenny, who had always been cool and calm, was now so distressed and I also think she was drinking much more than ever.

"Karen, I'm afraid of this man, and I don't know what to do," "she said. "I don't have any money left to get out of this. Tip will hide everything."

Apparently, Tip was cruel, with a violent streak. Jenny was stuck in a mess with no family left to help her out. My heart broke after seeing my once-brave friend so downtrodden, desperate, and helpless.

Jenny had been a strong woman back when we lived in Hollywood, so full of life and sure of herself and her talent. She had the whole world in front of her, but both her Hollywood marriages left her broken.

Leonard would call me about a year later with the news that Jenny had been murdered. It was on the news and in the papers. She had separated from Tip and filed for divorce. She was living in an apartment in Beverly Hills. After having some minor surgery, Tip picked her up from the hospital to take her back to her apartment.

The two were shot while waiting for the elevator in the lobby of Jenny's building. Since Jenny died first, Tip inherited anything Jenny had. Tip's daughters took everything, and Brian, Jenny's son, ended up with nothing of Jenny's. They would not even give him back his old dirt bike.

There were no witnesses, and at first, the police thought it was a random shooting.

Later, it was revealed that Tip had been involved with a few of the mob guys who hung out at Trackton's, a well-known restaurant on La Cienega Boulevard. The shooter had been provided guns that were in the back of the trunk of Tip's car. The guy was supposed to go to Tip's car, get a gun and kill Jenny. The plan was also to wound Tip, but the guy probably decided that Tip might name him and decided to make his shot a fatal one. He killed them both.

I later heard from Buddy Moorehouse, a cousin of Jenny's who wrote the book, "Murder of an Elvis Girl: Solving the Jenny Maxwell Case."

Apparently, Tip had previously tried to hire three guys to kill Jenny. One was an ex-cop who had gotten into trouble. The file has been re-opened, but they concluded that the shooter was probably an out-of-town hire and would be too difficult to find. No one would be charged with killing Jenny and Tip.

Leonard would take me up to Gene Roddenberry's house one evening, where I would meet his wife, Majel. I was sitting on the couch talking to Majel while we drank our glasses of wine. Leonard was in the other room on the phone. I don't know why, but I got up and walked to the window overlooking the pool, where the lights lit up the water while Majel still sat on the couch at the other end of the room.

Looking down at the pool, I saw two figures madly making love in the blue-lit water; it was Gene and a blonde. I don't know why I ever opened my mouth and said something; I probably shouldn't have, but I did. I turned to where Majel sat, and in a shocked voice, I said, "Majel, do you know Gene is in the pool having sex with another woman?"

Majel nodded and raised her wine glass.

"What can I do?" she said.

I thought back at my Hollywood days and how so many men with everything a beautiful wife would offer always looked elsewhere. Enough was never enough. This was the choice she had made, the same as many other wives with husbands in the business.

INSIGHTS

I knew it wasn't just this town. I thought perhaps things might be better elsewhere, but sadly enough, elsewhere would bring other problems.

Men would be insecure knowing I had dated Elvis or Warren. It was insecurity that sometimes couldn't be overcome with actions or words, no matter how much you might love them. Beauty does come with a price, regardless of what you may hear.

Monsters who corrupt the lives of young girls do not just live in Hollywood; they hide out in small, unknown towns, the names of which you may have never heard.

Hollywood was a dream for me, and I chose to leave it behind when it appeared it was being fulfilled. I would have to decide when my next dream would begin.

EPILOGUE: SWEETIE

One night in 1985, Sweetie said to me, "Honey, I'm going to be moving."

"Where are you going to move to," I asked her.

"Maybe Hollywood, dear," she said. "Will you help me, honey? I said I would.

Sweetie had dementia, and the family had been taking turns staying with her at night.

Weeks later, I sat by her side and held her hand. She had become comatose. Lorna was in the kitchen; Doug was there earlier. My mother was on her way.

I sat there, talking to her while pushing back her hair from her forehead as she became restless. I told her my mother would soon be there, which seemed to calm her down.

After my mother arrived and spent a few minutes with Sweetie, I took a break and went into the kitchen. Lorna was making lunch for my mother and me. I went to the refrigerator and grabbed a soda, and passed my mother in the hallway as she was leaving Sweetie's room to get a cup of coffee and catch up with Lorna in the kitchen.

Sweetie seemed calm as I sat down next to her. I reached for her hand and started talking to her again, going back over the past. I thanked her for all the wonderful times she had been there for me. I told her how much I had loved our

Christmases with the family all together and the darling, short, fat trees that she preferred.

Those trees were special. She'd carefully unwrap the decorations that had been her mother's and hung them on the tree. I helped with the tinsel that would dance once the colored lights were added.

I saw a slight movement at the corners of her lips, as if a smile was trying to appear.

"Sweetie, you can go now," I said to her. "I am here with you."

She took a shallow breath, and then a rush coursed through my body. It was so sudden and so swift; it was almost as if I had been struck by lightning.

She was gone, and I had been there to help her move, just as she had asked, and I had been given the gift of feeling her spirit pass through me as she left us. After getting myself together, I realized it really was a beautiful blessing to have been chosen by her to share her last moments on earth.

MALIBU – 2023

It was a beautiful, hot, sunny day as I got in my car and rolled down the windows. It was a perfect day for the beach. I had planned to take the freeways to hit Sunset Boulevard off the I-605, then take it down to the coast to reach my destination in Malibu for lunch.

I had made plans to meet up with the actress Rosemary Forsyth, who I knew from my Kitty Jones Lee days.

The memories of the old Hollywood days came rushing back. I yearned to see if the old Sunset Strip looked anything like it had back then.

I decided to leave the Ventura freeway and get off before reaching the I-605 so I could go over Laurel Canyon and down the hill to the old turn-off I used to make on Lookout Mt., the street that once led me to Jenny Maxwell's house, and further up the winding street near the top, where Jimmy Mitchum once lived. And halfway up was Budd Albright's little place on the left.

I put those memories behind me as I turned right onto Sunset Boulevard. I caught a glance of where the old Schwab's Pharmacy once was; now, a Cineplex fills the whole corner. I knew Pandora's Box had been gone for quite a few years. Further down the strip, so much of the past was changed, but then I found The Body Shop had survived all these years, and the Whiskey A Go Go was still rocking away on the corner of Clark and Sunset; sadly, the Hamburger Hamlet was gone.

I drove further along Sunset Boulevard, heading to the Pacific Palisades to hit Hwy. 1, where I would first see the gorgeous view of the sun sparkling on the ocean, and feel the sense of peace come over me as it always had years before when I would take this same drive.

I looked back at the days and life I'd left behind and smiled, knowing I was content with my life and the choices I made. I have no regrets, and I had a lifetime of wonderful memories that could never have happened without escaping a life I knew could be better. It's not easy to take chances, but if you don't, you will always live with the what ifs. I'd like to think my gypsy soul gave me the wisdom to know when it was time to end one dream and the courage to begin another.

By the way, I had Sweetie's ring on my finger and can now truly say I did help Sweetie go to Hollywood.

PHOTO CREDITS

PANORAMA TERRACE, BONNIE CONRAD, ROBIN and CHRIS POLLOCK: Courtesy of the Karlyle Family.

BURGER HAMLET and RAT PACK-barstool 1960: Copyright permission is given by Bison Archives and HollywoodHistorialPhotos.com.

BATMAN and OSCAR GRAPHIC Copyright Permission given by Shutterstock.

BONNIE BOYD, aka BONNIE KARLYLE SWANK COVER PHOTO: Courtesy of the Bernard Of Hollywood Photography. Copyright Permission was given by: Grandson, Joshua John Miller

KAREN CONRAD and daughter ROBIN POLLOCK JACOBS and SAMUEL FULLER'S AUTOGRAPHED PHOTO to KAREN CONRAD: Courtesy of Bonnie Karlyle.

WEDDING DINNER PHOTO-Clint Eastwood, Maggie Eastwood, Kitty Lee Jones, Richard Lee, James Brolin and wife Jane and PHOTO OF KITTY LEE JONES and CLINT EASTWOOD: Courtesy of the Richard Lee Family.

DAVID SOUL, BONNIE KARLYLE, CLINT EASTWOOD: Courtesy of Bonnie Karlyle

JENNEY MAXWELL: Courtesy of the Buddy Morehouse family.

KART MAGAZINE PHOTO and PHOTO of Steve Rowland, Kitty Lee, and Budd Albright: Courtesy of Budd Albright.

LOS ANGELES "CLEOPATRA" PREMIERE 1963 - Found on Martin Turnbull's website: Garden of Allah

JIM MITCHUM AND KAREN CONRAD PHOTO: Courtesy of the family of Norma B. Boyd.

VIC MORROW - Public Domain

YUL BRYNNER - Anna and the King Television 1972: Copyright Permission given by: Historic Collection Almay Stock Photo.

"ROUSTABOUT" 1965 British advertisement for the Elvis Presley Movie: Copyright Permission given by: Historic collection /Almay Stock Photo.

ABOUT THE AUTHOR

Bonnie Karlyle, aka Karen Conrad, still lives in the L.A. area. After she left Hollywood, she re-married and had two more sons. She developed her practical side by becoming an Escrow Officer but needed to embrace her creativity by designing and making jewelry.

In 1980, she moved from Palm Desert, CA, back to the Hollywood/San Fernando Valley area, entering the Music Business as a songwriter and writing for a songwriter's publication.

She had her first record, "Sabotage My Heart," in which she wrote the lyrics recorded by Shannon. Next came "No Promise-No Guarantee," again her lyric, recorded by Laura Brannigan.

She wrote the words and music to the title song "Forever" by Chapter 8, Anita Baker's original group, along with "Stand Back, Take a Look," recorded by E.Q for Atlantic Records.

Her last recording with her lyric, "A Dream with Your Name on It," was recorded by Jennifer Holliday, which led to Billy Porter's Star Search, 'Star of the Year,' winning with the song in 1990.

In 2022 Apple T.V.'s series "DEAR" starred Billy Porter and used the song in that episode.

Still feeling that creative urge, she decided to write this book at the urging of her son, Michael.